David & Linda MacKinnon

Homemaking Programs, Talks and Activities

written by Nyla Witmore

STANDARD PUBLISHING
Cincinnati, Ohio   2973

Illustrations by Romilda Dilley

Unless otherwise noted, Scripture quotations are from the New American Standard Bible, © The Lockman Foundation 1960, 1962, 1963, 1968, 1971, 1972, 1973, 1975, and are used by permission.

Library of Congress Cataloging in Publication Data

Witmore, Nyla.
  Homemaking programs.

  1. Home economics—Study and teaching.
I. Title.
TX165.W55   640   82-5626
ISBN 0-87239-565-0   AACR2

© 1982, Nyla Jane Witmore

Published by The Standard Publishing Company
Cincinnati, Ohio
Division of Standex International Corporation
Printed in U.S.A.

Preface

In my grade-school and teen years I tried every way possible to get out of housework.

My lack of training was not my mother's fault. She tried. However, I preferred to socialize, play piano and think about boys. My excuses for not doing housework were usually some variation of the themes: "But, Mother, my studies are more important" or "I've got to practice my music for two hours every day." Yes, I was convinced my piano and my studies needed me more than the dust balls multiplying under my bed.

Then came college and suddenly I thought, *What if I don't end up as a teacher for the rest of my life? What if I get married?*

Convinced I would flunk "Domestic 101" the first two weeks of marriage, I decided to prepare for both eventualities. I majored in Speech and Speech Therapy and elected a Home and Family Living minor. This would, I reasoned, fill the void from my misspent years of domestic truancy.

Upon graduation I taught school for three years. For two of those years, I was a new bride. At the end of the third year, I retired to experience the birth of our first son, Michael. Never could I imagine I would love motherhood so much. Even more surprising was the fading of career urges. I had no desire to return to teaching Speech Therapy. (I realize that not all women have the same experience as I.)

Two years later, our second son, Christopher, was born. As the boys grew, I taught them to enjoy baking. They and their friends would don flimsy aprons and father's old shirts. I would line them up in front of the kitchen sink to inspect their hands. With a footstool placed in front of the sink well, each child had an opportunity to knead the bread dough ten times before relinquishing that position to wait at the end of the line for the second round of kneading. It was a great way to get my bread kneaded! The kids loved it and eagerly awaited the pleasure of sampling the hot, yeasty bread afterwards.

Eventually a group of women at the church asked me to share my single rise bread-making techniques with thirty teenage girls. The church women were sponsoring an outreach program to the community, teaching some of the arts of homemaking that were likely to be lost to future generations. I was happy to help out—for one session only.

After that one session, I found all sorts of excuses to "audit" the sessions taught by other women in the church. In ten weeks I learned to bake a flaky pie crust, knit a poncho of hairpin lace, decorate a cake, do decoupage, and polish silver.

Did the course make a difference? Ask my husband and two sons! They've had the benefit of my renewed excitement for domestic activity. I could never have learned all those skills from my mother alone. Thank God for the Christian women who pooled their resources to stimulate so many of us and provide insurance against domestic boredom.

I no longer think of a "homemaker" as someone who hangs around the house all day. No, I'm not on a "homemaker high" twenty-four hours a day, three hundred sixty-five days a year, and I cannot promise that you will be. But, as you participate in the meditations and activities in this book, I can promise that you'll discover things about yourself that will make you a richer, more interesting person.

—*The Author*

Table of Contents

How to Use This Book 6

Culinary Skills

1. Budget Cooking 13
2. Bread Baking 26
3. Cake Decorating 33
4. Pie Making 42

Crafts

5. Needlecrafts 56
6. Candle Making 75
7. Flower Arranging 81

You and Your Home

8. Good Grooming and Wardrobe Selection ... 95
9. Money Management 115
10. Simple Home Repairs 129
11. Caring for Silver, Linens and China 138
12. Entertaining at Home 151

How to Use This Book

Give us five good reasons for having a series of homemaking sessions for our women's group.

1. Because we recognize the need to preserve the family unit through which we can best teach moral and spiritual values.
2. Because we enjoy being with each other, yet we want to make our time together count for something beyond fellowship and good times.
3. Because we want to learn skills that can last a lifetime.
4. Because we recognize the arts and talents among our members which should not be lost to future generations.
5. Because none can be gifted in all areas of homemaking, we recognize the need to pool resources, to teach each other and to allow a vehicle by which the older can teach the younger.

How should we organize our group for these programs?

Use this chart to help you get organized. It's followed by hints for the various committee chairwomen.

1. Who will be in our group?_____
2. What will the age range be? _____
3. Daytime or evening sessions? _____
4. Size of each group?_____

5. How often to meet: Weekly?   Monthly?
6. How many sessions? (List them below.)

1. _____ Teacher _____
   name and date of session Helper _____
2. _____ Teacher _____
                          Helper _____
3. _____ Teacher _____
                          Helper _____
4. _____ Teacher _____
                          Helper _____
5. _____ Teacher _____
                          Helper _____
6. _____ Teacher _____
                          Helper _____
7. _____ Teacher _____
                          Helper _____
8. _____ Teacher _____
                          Helper _____
9. _____ Teacher _____
                          Helper _____
10. _____ Teacher _____
                          Helper _____
11. _____ Teacher _____
                          Helper _____
12. _____ Teacher _____
                          Helper _____

7. Committee Chairwomen

   General Director

   _____

   _____

   Recruiter (to schedule teachers/helpers)

   _____

   _____

   Publicity (news releases, posters)

   _____

   _____

   Registration

   _____

   _____

   Note: Two spaces are given for each category. Use one as a backup in case the first person declines. Or consider suggesting two persons become cochairwomen.

General Director (or Cochairwomen)

—Give yourself a deadline for the time you expect to have recruited all your workers, presenters, helpers, etc.
—One month before programs begin, call a general meeting of all workers to pass out schedules, job descriptions, etc.
—Be available by phone to help chairwomen think through their questions and problems.
—Anytime you delegate a job, try to write it down so you won't forget whom you asked. (This keeps slipups to a minimum and saves your sanity!)
—Always say, "I'll call you back on (day and time) to get an update."

Recruiter

—Brainstorm with your committee about the talents among your membership. Consider going outside your group for teachers with special skills. Keep a list of every name and possible idea.
—If the prospect says, "Oh, I could never get up in front of a group," ask, "Would you be willing to be a helper for the one who does?"
—If someone has needed abilities but is reluctant to teach, assure her that she doesn't have to be an authority on the subject. You want her to share what works for her. Remind your candidate that she can recruit an assistant to share the teaching role if she wishes.
—Once a week, call your General Director to give her an update.

Teachers

—You are there to share from your experience. Do not apologize for any lack of speaking skills.
—Many speakers find it is helpful to begin with an amusing anecdote or relate how they became interested in their subject.
—Point out those things that you think are absolutely essential. "What four things," for example, "should a person know before buying a new wardrobe?"
—List a few "no-nos" like, "There are three things you should watch out for if you're going to make candles at home."
—If you are asking questions of the group, compliment good thinking with such remarks as, "I'm so glad you brought that up," or "That's a very good question."
—If you sense your listeners are getting restless, ask a question. "Do you think that buying the cheapest brand is the best way to save money? Are there times when it isn't?"
—Practice your presentation at home once or twice before you speak. Use a mirror to help you.

Helpers

—Your job is to assist the teacher in securing supplies, helping to demonstrate, or aiding the women in hands-on activities.
—Arrive a half hour before session to help the teacher set up.
—Whenever possible, keep things running smoothly so that the teacher can speak without interruption.
—If the teacher or hostess has forgotten something and needs a "runner" to leave the premises, make sure that another helper will cover for you.

Evaluation Sheet

As our program series is drawing to a close, we ask you to help us plan for the success of future programs. You may turn this sheet in at the conclusion of the final session. (It is not necessary to sign your name.)

1. I enrolled in the homemaking group because _____
   _____.

2. I would be interested in attending follow-up sessions on _____.

3. Topics to be included in another series might be ____
   _____.

4. Was the time of year appropriate? yes ____ no ____

5. Was the day and time convenient? yes ____ no ____

6. A better time for me would have been _____.

7. The number of sessions was just right ____, too many ____, not enough ____.

8. ____ (number of sessions) would have been better.

9. I would recommend this series to my friends when it is offered again. yes ____ no ____
10. I am 16 or younger ____. I am 17 or older ____.
I am a working woman ____. I am single ____. I am a full-time homemaker ____.

Note: You may select from any of the above questions to prepare your own evaluation sheet. Try to keep all questions contained on a single sheet.

If you wish to use an evaluation sheet to help you recruit new members for future sessions, you could include a tear-off registration form at the bottom so participants could pass on the information to their friends.

What about pre-registration and early enrollment? Should we limit enrollment?

Pre-registration helps you plan ahead. To test your idea of using this series, you could arrange for a special presentation to your club or group, two or three months prior to the time when you would like to begin.

Make this a businesslike event. Don't simply ask for a show of hands. Have index cards available with space for persons to write down:
Name
Age
Address
Phone number
Special homemaking interests or skills

With this information in hand, you can then decide whether you have enough interest from your group to fill up a complete registration of no more than twenty persons. (Groups of fourteen to sixteen are ideal. If more than twenty express interest, plan to have two or more separate groups.)

Suppose you have only ten volunteers with early interest. Go back to the planning committee and consider, "Should we open the enrollment to others in the community at large?" This might make an excellent outreach program. Consider also including teenage girls in your groups; they are the homemakers of tomorrow!

Early enrollment helps you plan for the purchase of supplies. A merchant is more apt to give you a discount if you will be purchasing for a group of ten or more.

Early enrollment helps you determine the "person power" needed to conduct each session so you can do a better job of recruiting workers.

How early can we begin advertising?

The first advertising begins the moment you decide to have a homemaking series. Talk it up among your friends. Let enthusiasm begin to bubble and then begin tentative recruitment of workers.

Enrolling is a subtle form of advertising. Six weeks before you begin classes, begin enrolling members.

Put up signs and posters in your church or meeting place a week or so before you begin the actual registration. Local merchants and businesses might be willing to let you display a small poster.

Newspaper advertising can start with an advance notice of your intent to hold a series. Then four weeks before classes start, begin a serious campaign that includes more details. You'll want to mention specific classes and the persons who will be teaching them. (Some newspapers get cramped for space and may request that you limit your advertising to one notice two weeks prior and again one week before programs begin.)

CHAPTER 1

Budget Cooking

CHALLENGING THE HEART

A number of years ago in southern California, a whale washed up on the beach. Many men worked all night to get the whale on a truck to transfer it. Not an easy task! Finally, with the whale loaded, they began the uphill drive from the beach area. Suddenly the whale started slipping. It slid from the truck and into a house. It was 2:00 a.m. when those living in the house were awakened by the sound of plate glass breaking. "Our picture window is ruined!" the homeowner shouted as he and his wife came outside to survey the damage. Rubbing their eyes, they reportedly said, "Maybe if we go back to bed, it'll go away."

Problems are like whales in our living rooms. We hope that by ignoring difficulties, they will go away.

Consider the problem of feeding the starving people in the world. When our tummies are full, we find it easier to suggest that the Red Cross or another charitable group send supplies. We may give a few dollars to missionaries or relief agencies, but we still find it hard to imagine the personal pain of starvation and malnutrition.

Suppose, however, that you were living on a strict budget. (Most of us today are!) Again you might say, "I can't afford to help those people. I have to feed my own family!"

Using some of the ideas in this week's budget cooking class, plan to have a nutritious but no-frills "Third World" meal—perhaps just rice to which you have added nuts, legumes, beans, or vegetables. Then, take the money you would normally spend on a hearty meat-and-potatoes dinner or a meal at the local fast-food restaurant and give that money to a missionary or world relief agency.

It is hard to imagine that California man hoarding the whale. Even if his wife were a fantastic cook, there would be only so many ways to cook whale burgers, whale steaks, whale goulash, whale soup or whale soufflé! What at first might appear to be a bountiful blessing of food would eventually turn into a bountiful stink. That's the way it is with too much of anything.

Consider the story of the rich man that Jesus Christ told as a lesson to His followers (Luke 12:16-21). A rich man had land that bore good crops. He began to think to himself, *I don't have a place to keep all my crops. What can I do? I will store my grain and all my other goods. Then I will say to myself,* "You lucky man! You have all the good things you need for many years. Take life easy. Eat! Drink! Enjoy yourself!" But God said to him, "You fool! This very night you will have to give up your life. Then who will get all these things you have kept for yourself?" Afterwards Jesus concluded, "So it is with those who pile up riches for themselves but are not rich in God's sight."

What are your "riches?" Lots of pretty clothes? Lots of friends? Plenty to eat? Good grades at school? Good job? Make sure you don't spend these only on yourself. Let your good things in life be used to benefit others.

Prayer: Sometimes I have a hard time recognizing the wealth and good things I already have. I'm often more concerned with how much more I can get. How I need to see beyond what gives me pleasure! God, help my heart to feel the needs of others more each day. Amen.

CHALLENGING THE HANDS

Suggested Activities

1. As a class, put together a "master mix" (see recipes in this chapter). Divide into groups to make different goodies from the same mix.

2. Invite an expert to teach safe canning or freezing. (County Extension Services may be able to help you.) If you have access to a large farmer's market or can arrange to buy in bulk from your grocer, you can select high-grade products at reduced prices. If you grow your own, all the better. Each person could take home one or two jars of the things made.

3. Have a coupon cutting and trading night. Make use of magazines and scissors and ingenuity. Learn how to make coupons pay in savings. Divide into teams and see how much your group has been able to save by the end of the course. One women's magazine regularly carries a feature for coupon cutters; begin searching magazines for clues to better money management with coupons. (And remember, the item you buy isn't a true savings unless it's an item you will use.)

4. Invite a doctor or nutrition expert to discuss meal planning and dieting.

What is a good basic diet?

You can remember this easily by thinking 2-2-4-4.
- 2—meat group (meat, fish, poultry, eggs)
- 2—milk group (milk, cheese, ice cream). Although the body needs calcium, it is questioned how much milk adults should consume. Adults may get calcium from other sources. Supplementation of bone meal may be helpful.
- 4—vegetables and fruits (including 1 citrus and 1 leafy green vegetable)
- 4—bread or cereal (part should be whole grains)

Each day's total food intake should include the 2-2-4-4 number of servings from the four basic food groups.

What did you have for breakfast? For dinner? Write it down. What basic nutrient source was missing? Could you get that nutrient in another meal during the day?

Just for fun, analyze this meal: chicken breast, mashed potatoes, applesauce, vanilla ice cream. It's all white, isn't it? White may be good for brides, but it's not good for the decor on your dinner plate. What's wrong with white? First, it's boring. Second, white may suggest you have too much starch in your meal. In this case mashed potatoes and applesauce are both starches.

What could help this meal? Think Christmas! Get some red and green in there. A red tomato and some leafy greens will not only perk up the appearance of the meal, but it will satisfy the requirement of having at least one citrus and one leafy green vegetable. Now you have better balance and beauty.

It is said that American diets are too heavy in red meat, sugar, white flour, and salt. How can we improve our diets?

Instead of having red meat five days a week, consider the following: lean beef or pork twice a week, fish twice, poultry twice, and one meatless but complete protein meal. What is a complete protein? According to Frances Lappe in her book *Diet for a Small Planet,* complementary proteins that give a proper balance of amino acids are:

   Legumes + Rice
   Soybeans + Rice + Wheat
   Beans + Wheat
   Soybeans + Corn + Milk
   Beans + Corn
   Soybeans + Wheat + Sesame
   Milk + Beans
   Soybeans + Peanuts + Sesame
   Wheat + Rice
   Soybeans + Sesame + Wheat

This means a meatless meal doesn't have to be lacking in essential proteins. It is combinations of the above that nutritionists consider when feeding Third World countries who do not have abundant supplies of poultry, fish, etc. (See also *Recipes for a Small Planet* by Ellen Ewald. Both are paperbacks published by Ballantine/Cookbook.)

There is much controversy over "sugars" in general. Refined white sugar is the most criticized. We would all do well to cut down or eliminate our dependency on sweeteners. Sugar sneaks into everything—coating mixes, packaged sauces, salad dressings, and cereals. Just read the labels on every box you buy this week. Watch out for words such as dextrose and corn syrup. They are sugars, too. If you wish to switch to a simple sugar (one that breaks down quickly in the body) choose fresh fruits.

Honey is an easily digested sugar; the bees have already done some digesting for you. Dark honey is often strong in flavor while the light is milder. If you are going to use honey in cooking, choose milder flavors so they won't overpower your recipe. When substituting honey for sugar, follow this guide: Use ¾ cup of honey for each 1 cup of sugar.

If you love salt, you know how hard it is to cut back. If you have a "salt tooth," consider using garlic powder or onion as flavorings. You won't miss the absence of salt as much.

Unbleached flour is preferable to white, according to some sources, because it escapes one step in chemical processing that may rob it of nutrients. Or, if you can find a specialty store that grinds grain or offers a wide variety of flours, consider buying whole wheat pastry flour. The consistency is closer to white flour than is ordinary whole wheat flour, and it substitutes more successfully in your recipes.

The old rule says to drink six to eight glasses of water a day. Isn't that a lot?

Even if you are dieting—in fact, especially if you are dieting—you need more water than you realize. Water is to the body what water in the radiator is to a car. It flushes impurities from the system. It keeps you from overheating on a hot day. And for the dieting person, water makes you feel fuller and less apt to be tempted by junk foods, white breads and pastries. Whenever you crave food, go have a glass of water—no calories, either!

Is it true that you should eat foods closest to their natural state?

Raw or slightly cooked vegetables and fruits are the most nutritious. They also retain their color well. Vegetables should be cooked to the "just tender" stage. Steamed vegetables are the most beautiful of all. Save any liquid and store it in a jar in your refrigerator. It makes great soup stock.

Consider cooking poultry, meats, and other protein foods under the "low and slow" guideline. That means, cook on low heat for longer periods of time. Meat will shrink less, the eggs will stay firm, and you won't have tough meat or rubbery eggs. Wean yourself away from well-done steaks. In reality, they're probably overcooked, and you're throwing money down the drain.

Are there times when you should cook foods at high temperatures?

Stir-fry and wok cooking is becoming increasingly popular. The secret to high heat cookery is to get the oil hot enough to cook the food in a short period of time. Never cook anything on high heat for long periods. If you are cooking vegetables under high heat, add first those vegetables that are known to take longer, such as carrots and green beans. Cook those a few minutes before adding green peppers, celery, and onions. Most American cooking puts onions in first. Not so in Oriental dishes. The onions are cooked last because they cook the quickest.

How can I know if I'm getting the best and most economical purchase? Are the cheapest items necessarily the most economical?

Cheese used to be a great penny-pinching food. No longer. Once people started flocking to the dairy counters, the prices went up. What is one year's bargain find may become another year's luxury, so you need to read the food ads to get the best price per pound or per serving. Stock up on "specials" at the store.

Usually an economy roast that is braised (cooked at low temperatures in liquid or broth) will turn out tender and at the same time will be kind to your purse. Watch for sales, and then buy and freeze.

Regarding ground meats, the cheapest price isn't always the best. Check the package to see what percentage of fat is included in plain ground beef. Compare that with extra-lean or ground round. If you want to be sure your meat will not shrink away to nothing, you might want to pay for a higher priced ground meat. Some fat in any cut of meat will help the flavor and keep meat tender, but avoid those cuts which result in pounds of fat going down the drain.

Another way to be sure you are getting the best value is to check the label on the grocery counter for unit cost. Some stores are indicating cost per serving, which is an even greater help. You can be sure the items with highest cost per unit will be placed at eye level, so check the top and bottom shelves for other brands.

Never shop without a list. If children beg for items, say, "I will check and see if it's on my list. If not, we'll get it the next time." This stops lots of crying and helps you both be in greater control of impulses to buy. Be aware that grocers put their "impulse" items at the ends of aisles.

Never shop on an empty stomach! You'd be surprised what you think you can't live without when your stomach is growling.

What about cooking food in batches?

Some women find that spending a Saturday cooking multiple dishes is a great way to cut down time in the kitchen during the rest of the week. Others like to cook on Thursday or Friday so they won't have to spend so much time apart from the family on weekends. The idea of "three from one" recipes is a good way to get the most meals from the initial time spent cooking. You prepare a "master mix" and follow the recipes for variations. Here are some to help you get started.

READY HAMBURGER MIX*

4 lbs. lean ground beef
1 large onion
2 teaspoons salt
½ teaspoon pepper
½ teaspoon oregano
¼ teaspoon garlic salt

Brown beef; add onion. Cook together until onions are golden. Drain fat. Add remaining ingredients. Cool; spoon into four 1-pint freezer containers (leave ½ inch at top). Freeze for use within 3 months.

TACO SALAD* using Ready Hamburger Mix
(serves 8)

2 cups Ready Hamburger Mix thawed
1 (7 oz.) can green chili salsa
1 head lettuce torn in bite-size pieces
3 large tomatoes, chopped
1 large avocado, chopped (optional)
4-5 green onions, chopped
2 cups grated cheddar cheese
1 (15 oz.) can kidney beans, drained
1 (10 oz.) pkg. tortilla chips
Salad dressing of your choice

Combine Mix with chili salsa in medium skillet and heat through. In large salad bowl combine next 6 ingredients. Add hamburger mixture and toss gently. Add tortilla chips and top with salad dressing of your choice.

This dish is great for a hot summer night. See the bright color and complete use of protein, vegetable, grain, and citrus?

SATURDAY STROGANOFF* using Ready Hamburger Mix (4-6 servings)

2 cups Ready Hamburger Mix
1 (10¾ oz.) can cream of celery soup, condensed
1 (10¾ oz.) can cream of mushroom soup, condensed
¾ cup milk
1 pint sour cream
cooked noodles
poppy seeds for garnish

Combine and heat hamburger, soups and milk. Simmer about 10 minutes. Just before serving add the sour cream and simmer 2 minutes longer.
Serve over cooked noodles and garnish with poppy seeds if desired.

SPAGHETTI CASSEROLE* using Ready Hamburger Mix (6-8 servings)

Preheat oven to 350°

1 (12 oz.) pkg. spaghetti, cooked according to package directions
3 cups grated cheddar cheese
1 pint Ready Hamburger Mix
1 (2¼ oz.) can mushrooms
1 (10½ oz.) can condensed tomato soup
½ cup milk
1 (15 oz.) jar spaghetti sauce

In bottom of buttered 2½ to 3 quart casserole, place half of the cooked spaghetti. Sprinkle half the grated cheese on spaghetti. Place half of Ready Hamburger Mix on top of cheese. Add layer of half of the mushrooms. Repeat the layers.
In small bowl, combine tomato soup, milk, spaghetti sauce, and pour over entire casserole. Add more milk during baking if needed to keep casserole moist.
Bake 1 hour until bubbly.

QUICK MIX* for Cakes, Pancakes, Biscuits, Cookies
(makes 13 cups)

8½ cups unbleached flour
1 tablespoon baking powder
1 tablespoon salt
2 teaspoons cream of tartar
1 teaspoon baking soda
1½ cups instant nonfat dry milk
2¼ cups vegetable shortening

Sift all dry ingredients together. Blend well. Cut in shortening with pastry blender until evenly distributed (mixture will resemble cornmeal).
Store in large, airtight containers. Label for use within 10-12 weeks.

APPLE-NUT CAKE* using Quick Mix
(makes one 8-inch cake)

Preheat oven to 375°. Lightly grease an 8-inch square pan.

2⅓ cups Quick Mix
1 cup brown sugar, firmly packed
1 teaspoon cinnamon
½ teaspoon ground cloves
2 eggs slightly beaten
¼ cup milk or water
2 cups pared, cored, and grated apples
½ cup raisins
½ cup chopped nuts

In medium bowl combine Mix, brown sugar, cinnamon, cloves. Mix well and add eggs and milk. Blend with electric mixer for 1 minute. Add apples and blend 2 more minutes. Stir in raisins and nuts.
Pour into prepared pan. Bake 40-50 minutes until toothpick inserted in center comes out clean. Cool in pan 10 minutes; then cool on wire rack.

For variation, try Banana-Nut Cake: Omit raisins. Substitute 1 cup mashed bananas for apples.

NEVER-FAIL ROLLED BISCUITS* using Quick Mix
(makes 12 large biscuits)

Preheat oven to 450°.

3 cups Quick Mix
⅔ cup milk or water

    Combine above ingredients; let stand 5 minutes. On lightly floured board, knead dough 15 times. Roll out to ½ inch thickness. Cut with floured biscuit cutter. Place 2 inches apart on ungreased baking sheet.
    Bake 10-12 minutes until golden brown.

MOLASSES COOKIES* using Quick Mix
(makes approximately 30 cookies)

2 cups Quick Mix
¼ cup sugar
½ teaspoon cinnamon
½ teaspoon ginger
¼ teaspoon cloves
1 egg yolk
½ cup molasses
sugar

    In medium bowl combine Mix, sugar, cinnamon, ginger, cloves; mix well. Combine egg yolk and molasses in small bowl. Add to dry ingredients. Blend and refrigerate at least one hour.
    Preheat oven to 375° and lightly grease baking sheets. Shape dough into 1½ inch balls; roll in sugar. Place on baking sheets; flatten with bottom of glass.
    Bake 8-10 minutes till edges are browned.

PANCAKES* using Quick Mix
(makes 10-12 4-inch pancakes or 3 large waffles)

2¼ cups Quick Mix
1 tablespoon sugar
1 egg
1½ cups milk or water

Combine Mix and sugar in medium bowl. Mix well. Combine egg and milk (or water) in small bowl. Add to dry ingredients. Blend well. Let stand 5-10 minutes.
Cook on hot oiled griddle 3-4 minutes. Flip only once.

* Recipes from *Make-A-Mix Cookery*; H.P. Books, Tucson, AZ. Used by permission.

More Budget Tips

1. When possible, cook more than one portion or recipe at a time. Freeze one for later use.

2. You can save both time and money when you shop by using the perimeter rule. The basic essentials of milk, bread, vegetables, fruits, and meats are usually located on the outside walls or aisles of your supermarket. Stay away from those middle aisles!

3. Find one or two favorite grocery stores and stick with them. Because you know the store layout, you will be less likely to yield to impulse buying and will tend to buy only those things you use regularly.

4. The distance you drive costs money too. Shopping at two or three different stores on grocery day may not be a savings.

5. Shop late Saturday evening to bargain for produce that might otherwise "go bad" over the weekend. Both you and the grocer will benefit.

6. Buy wilted and past-its-peak produce at bargain prices for use in soups.

7. Consider joining a food-buying cooperative if your family eats a lot of fruits and vegetables, and you know that bulk buying will not mean foods will go to waste because they can't be consumed quickly enough. Extend the life of nuts, grains, flours, by storing them in airtight containers in refrigerator or freezer.

8. Consider bulk buying of canned goods. Get neighbors or friends to join you. Some grocers are willing to sell large quantities for a modest discount; some grocery warehouse-type stores sell at discount all the time.

9. Remember, a bargain isn't a bargain unless you can really use it. If it's something you use regularly, of course it's a bargain. If it's something you *might* use someday, think twice about it.

CHAPTER 2

Bread Baking

CHALLENGING THE HEART

" 'I say to you, it is not Moses who has given you the bread out of heaven, but it is My Father who gives you the true bread out of heaven. For the bread of God is that which comes down out of heaven, and gives life to the world.' They said therefore to Him, 'Lord, evermore give us this bread.' Jesus said to them, 'I am the bread of life; he who comes to Me shall not hunger, and he who believes in Me shall never thirst' " (John 6:32-35).

Tonight we are going to learn about the significance of leavened and unleavened bread.

According to one definition from the dictionary, leaven is any substance (like yeast) that causes fermentation and the eventual rising of dough. Fermentation is the gradual giving off of bubbles of gas—a slow chemical decomposition.

Without leaven you have a flat, cracker-like bread. Matzo bread is a good example. Most people find that the flavor and appearance of bread is better when it has been leavened.

In the Old Testament days of Moses, the Israelites were given a command about eating unleavened bread. At that time the Jews were slaves in Egypt. When God asked the people to eat unleavened bread for seven days and to kill a spotless lamb whose blood they would paint on the doorposts of their homes, the Jews obeyed. God was about to unleash the last plague on Egypt. If God saw the blood on the doorposts, He would pass over. But in all other homes, the oldest son would die. Since Pharaoh's door did not carry the blood, his firstborn son died. Finally, his cold heart warmed enough to give the Israelites their freedom from bondage. To this day Jews celebrate a Passover feast in memory of that event.

Did you know that when Jesus and His disciples were together for their last supper that they were celebrating the Passover feast we just spoke of? This time, however, Jesus drew their attention to the similarities between His blood and the blood of the Passover lamb. He was trying to tell them that the new covenant was to replace the old covenant. Actually, the new covenant was the fulfillment of the old.

In 1 Corinthians 5:7, 8 it says, "For Christ our Passover also has been sacrificed. Let us therefore celebrate the feast." Paul also taught us that whenever we drink of the cup and eat of the bread of Communion, we are proclaiming Christ's death until He comes again.

Now let's look at the nature of leavening. One dictionary says that leaven is "an influence that silently spreads; has the power to change conditions or opinions." Isn't that just what Jesus does to our lives? Inside us He is silently spreading to change our lives.

Leaven, the dictionary says, has the power to spread through and transform. Yes, even our appearance is transformed when we let Jesus influence and rule our lives.

If you are a believer today, what are the telltale signs? Our "yeast" should be apparent. The influence of Christ in our lives should serve as "leaven" or "spiritual yeast" in the lives of our families and friends.

Prayer: As I knead the bread this day, remind me of the ways that I can be "yeast" to those around me. Amen.

CHALLENGING THE HANDS

The traditional method of baking bread involves four hours or more of preparation, since the bread must rise, be punched down, rise again, be punched down, then rise again in loaf pans. We will use a modern single rise method that is much quicker.

You'll love this recipe. It is great for those with only an hour or so of time, for those with little children underfoot, or for those who anticipate interruptions. This recipe was developed from the original International Multifoods CoolRise method.

If you mix up the bread dough the night before a special dinner, you will be sure to get considerable applause for being able to serve steaming hot bread with the meal. Since the bread sits in the refrigerator overnight and continues to rise, you can busy yourself with other things. Think what a surprise you could enjoy on Easter or Christmas morning—freshly baked bread!

Teacher's Note: Besides bringing the ingredients for a demonstration of bread making, you'll want to have a couple loaves baking during class so your students can sample the finished product.

Bring to class:
- mixing bowl (to hold 7 cups of dough)
- measuring cup
- measuring spoons
- rolling pin
- hand mixer (optional)
- wooden spoon
- waxed paper
- 1 terry cloth hand towel (to lay over bread to keep warm)
- 2 medium-size plastic bags or 1 large plastic bag (This will become a "hothouse" for the loaves when they are placed in the refrigerator to rise.)
- 1 apron or old shirt

2 regular-size bread loaf pans
1 pastry cloth or sheet for rolling out the bread

That's it for equipment. Now for the food supplies. If you measure items ahead of time and bring them in little plastic bags or jars, it takes up less space and time.

2 pkgs. active dry yeast
1 envelope instant dry milk (to make one quart). You will use only half of the envelope. Bread tastes the same without milk, but the nutritional value is higher if you include it.
3 tablespoons salad oil
2 tablespoons honey
1 tablespoon salt
5½ to 7 cups of white flour (I prefer unbleached flour.)

A word of caution . . . love your bread and it'll love you. Don't kill or punch your dough viciously. Treat it like a new baby, and I guarantee you'll have smooth, light bread.

STEP 1

- In a mixing bowl put ½ cup lukewarm water. (Not too hot or you'll kill the yeast! Test it on the inside of your wrist.)
- Add 2 pkgs. yeast.
- Mix until well dissolved.
- Add 1¾ cups warm (NOT HOT) water.
- Stir in half the packet of instant milk.
- Measure ONLY 2 tablespoons of oil and add to the above mixture.
- Add 1 tablespoon of salt.
- Add 2 tablespoons of honey.
- Let sit for 10 minutes or until bubbles begin to form around edges.

STEP 2

- Add 2 cups of the flour and beat (yes, I said beat) with mixer for 1 minute.

- Add 1 more cup of flour. Now use spoon to stir until smooth.
- Gradually add the remaining 2½ cups of flour.
- Knead dough for 5-10 minutes. (You may need more flour as you go along. You'll know your bread is just right when the dough becomes smooth, elastic and shiny.)

Hint: If you set a large mixing bowl on a low table or in the well of your sink, you can knead the bread right in the bowl. I knead it once—turn one quarter turn—knead again—turn, etc. It keeps the table from getting so messy.

STEP 3

- Cover your smooth, round blob of dough (dough in the mixing bowl please) with a towel.
- Let rise at room temperature for 20 minutes. (If you live in a cold climate, set a pan of hot water in the bottom of your oven. Put the mixing bowl on a rack and close the door.) In an emergency once I had to put the bread in the refrigerator at this point. The bread still turned out all right. This bread is hard to ruin. What a comfort!
- Punch the bread down to remove excess air bubbles.
- Divide into two equal loaves.
- Make the loaves by using a rolling pin to roll out dough to an 8 x 10 rectangle (approximately). This presses out air bubbles.
- With fingers, start rolling at one end. Squeeze tightly to remove still more air bubbles. Keep rolling till the end.
- Turn the ends under to make the loaf neat in appearance.
- Oil the loaf pans.
- Put bread into pans and oil the top of each loaf.
- Now oil one side of a sheet of waxed paper and place directly on top of the loaf.
- Place these loaf pans inside the large plastic bag. Pronounce a benediction over the loaves—something like "rest in peace" or "rise in peace"—and place loaves in refrigerator for 2-24 hours.

Note: At this point, you'll be ready to take your loaves home to rise in the refrigerator.

STEP 4

- After 2-24 hours have elapsed (no less than 2 hours please), it is time to bake. Set oven at 350° for metal pans or 325° for glass pans.
- Remove plastic bag and wax paper. Let loaves sit on counter for at least 20 minutes while oven heats up.
- Bake for 25-40 minutes till loaf is brown and sounds hollow when you tap the top.
- Place on cooling rack for a few minutes, then turn pans on side to tap out the loaf. Tap the bottom of the loaf, too. If it is not cooked enough the bottom will appear "gummy." Now butter up and enjoy!

HOW TO KNEAD BREAD*

1. Push away.

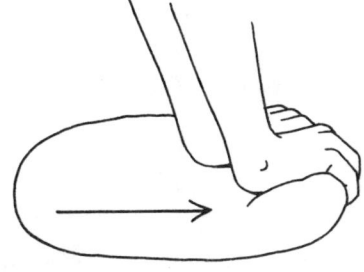

2. Fold dough over itself.

3. Repeat again and again.

4. Turn dough one quarter turn. Repeat steps 1-4 for at least 10-12 minutes.

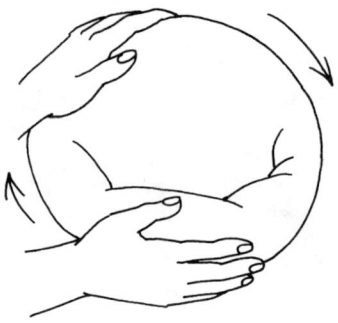

Cut open the dough with a knife. If you see big holes you need to knead some more!

*Reprinted from *BREAD SCULPTURE, THE EDIBLE ART,* © 1975 by Ann Wiseman, by permission of the publishers 101 Productions, San Francisco.

CHAPTER 3

Cake Decorating

CHALLENGING THE HEART

A little girl watched her mother mixing cake batter. It looked better than mud pies—soft, velvety and chocolate brown.

"Is it cake yet?" she asked.

"Not yet," her mother replied. "You have to wait."

The mother poured the batter into two round shiny pans. Then she bumped the pans on the counter top to bring air bubbles to the surface.

"Is it cake yet?" the little girl asked.

"No, dear, you'll have to wait a bit longer," the mother said.

Mother put the pans in the hot oven. The oven had a small window for watching things bake. The little girl got as close as Mother would allow. For a long time nothing seemed to be happening.

"I don't think it's ever going to be cake, Mommy," the little girl cried.

"Be patient. All good things are worth waiting for," the mother added knowingly.

Soon good smells were filling the room, a foretaste of good things to come. Looking inside the oven, the little girl could see the cake taking full shape.

"NOW, Mother, is it cake YET?"

Mother answered, "No, dear. If we take the cake out of the oven too early, the center may sink, and it will taste gooey."

Finally the exciting moment came. It was CAKE! Mother opened the oven door, carefully removed the cake to a wire cooling rack, and then set the table for a cake and milk snack.

The good things in life (God's best for us) are always the hardest things to wait for.

What are some of the things you have found it hard to wait for in your own life? First day of school? First date? Being on your own in an apartment? Getting your driver's license? That walk down the aisle as a bride? Your first baby? First important job? There will always be something just out of your grasp for which you yearn. Some yearn for greater patience. For more faith. For the assurance that God loves them. For forgiveness.

It is natural and normal to yearn. God knows that as long as we are on earth, we will never feel as if we're "cake" yet. We will always feel "unfinished." And that makes us impatient, doesn't it? Sometimes we are impatient with ourselves. Other times we are impatient with God.

In the book of Philippians, Paul has something encouraging to say to us about that. "I am confident of this very thing, that He who began a good work in you will perfect it until the day of Christ Jesus" (Philippians 1:6).

Prayer: Father, I get so impatient with myself. The good things I want to do, I often fail to do. The bad things I don't want to do, are often the things I am guilty of. Please hold a crown above my head and keep reminding me that one day, with Your help, I will grow into it. Give me the gift of "possibility thinking" so I can learn to see Your possibilities in me. Amen.

CHALLENGING THE HANDS

Suggested Activities

1. If your group is large and space limited, you may want to have one "demonstration cake" frosted by the leader. Two or three other cakes could be brought and frosted by teams of three or four. (Glaze cakes at home first. See instructions in this chapter.)

2. Ask each person to bring six cupcakes to frost and decorate.

3. A leader could demonstrate the unusual animal shapes that can be made from cutting long sheet cakes into appropriate pieces . . . then assembling . . . then frosting.

4. Each person could bring a box of dinner mints to decorate. In the winter, snowflakes, snowmen, and wreaths look nice and make a nice hostess gift. On Valentine's Day, mints can be decorated with hearts and flowers. Use your imagination!

5. Each person could bring a dozen baked cookies to decorate.

6. Each person can bring a batch of frosting from home or two or three batches of frosting can be made in class and shared among members.

If you are planning to invest in a small, basic kit of pastry tubes and various decorating tips, you will find them available in most craft shops or in the housewares and gourmet sections of large department stores.

It's best to start with the simple piping tube to get the feel of the pastry bag and learn how much pressure to use. After you've learned to master one tip, try a second. For the first few cakes, it's a good idea to use only one or two tips per cake. As you progress, you can learn more difficult techniques to make special flower and leaf shapes.

The best way to learn these techniques is to have someone show you and guide you every step of the way until you get the feel of it.

However, if you wish to do some simple home decorating for cookies, party mints, cupcakes, and cakes with a minimum of "on hand" supplies, here are some helpful suggestions:

BASIC SOFT FROSTING
(stays soft . . . good on cupcakes and cakes)

2 lbs. of confectioner's sugar
½ cup shortening
½ cup water or milk

Mix sugar and shortening; blend till smooth. Add liquid and beat until smooth.

Note: If you want your cakes and cupcakes to stay firm without crumbling when you spread them with frosting, glaze your cake first by diluting a small amount of the frosting mixture above. (Use just a few drops of water until it is an easy-to-spread consistency.) Set cake in refrigerator or freezer until ready to frost.

ICING THE CAKE*

1. Level cake: use sharp serrated knife in a sawing motion to remove uneven portions on each layer.

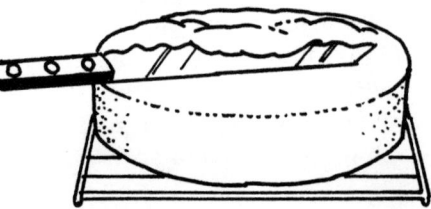

2. First layer: place bottom side upwards; it's the flattest. Spread frosting or jelly on top.

3. Add second layer with flattest side facing the first layer.

4. Slip small strips of wax paper under the bottom layer so frosting won't get your plate messy. (These can be pulled out when finished.)

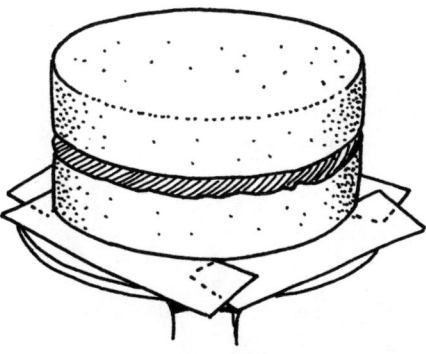

5. Frost top layer. Make a large mound in the center. Move from center toward edges, making sure the spatula touches only the icing, not the cake.

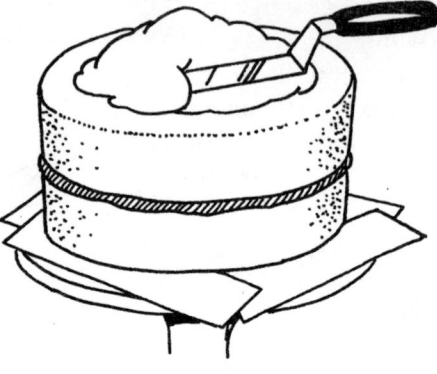

6. Spread excess from top to the sides. Then complete sides by holding spatula upright against the cake. Pressing lightly, turn the cake plate slowly with your free hand without lifting your spatula from cake surface.

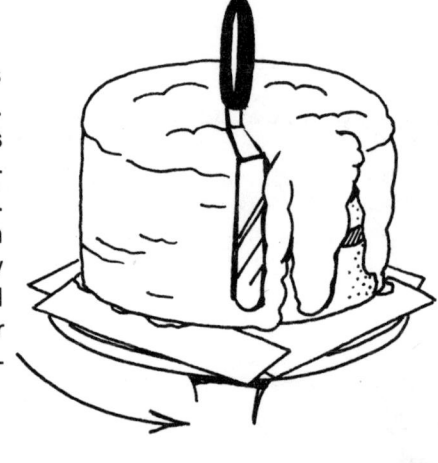

7. Smooth the surface on top and sides as necessary. (Do not run spatula under hot water to smooth icing.)

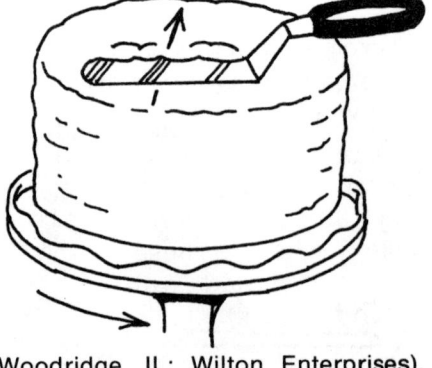

*Wilton Yearbook 1981. (Woodridge, IL: Wilton Enterprises), pg. 85.

DECORATING ICING
(with hard finish, for cookies, mints)

The frosting recipe that follows is easy to mix with the electric mixer and easy to apply with a plastic sandwich bag "tube."

2 egg whites
⅛ teaspoon cream of tartar
2 teaspoons water
2½ to 3 cups of sifted confectioner's sugar

Beat egg whites, cream of tartar and water till frothy. Gradually add powdered sugar. Beat until mixture holds soft peaks.

SANDWICH BAG DECORATING POUCH

Use the heavy sandwich bags with a zipper-like closure. With scissors, snip a tiny hole diagonally on one bottom corner. Fill bag about one-third full of frosting. Twist the bag to force all the frosting into the corner. You're ready to be artistic!

Using a slight pressure, you will see a small rope of frosting emerging from the end. Use this to write messages, outline a cookie, define areas, make dots.

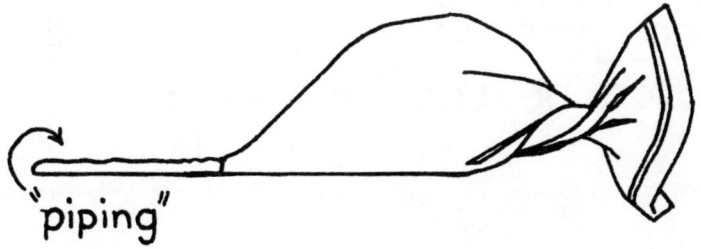

"dot"

Dinner mint dessert

Large cut in corner of pouch makes "big dots" for body; small cut makes "tiny dots" for features.

Red-pink-white Valentine cookies

Gingerbread boy

An easy way to use many colors is to put white frosting into two or three separate bags. Drop a different food coloring in each bag. Knead until the color is thoroughly mixed.

OTHER DECORATIONS

—Make marshmallow daisies! Wet scissors in hot water. Snip toward the center of the marshmallow to form five or six petals. Affix a yellow gumdrop center with a small amount of frosting. (Or use a toothpick to hold it securely on the cake . . . but warn guests!)

—Use colored mini-marshmallows to make designs.

—Make a design with M & M's.

—Dip string into food colors. Hold string taut and gently lay it across the top of white frosting cake. Then lift off. Repeat, using a variety of colors. Voila! A plaid cake!

CHAPTER 4

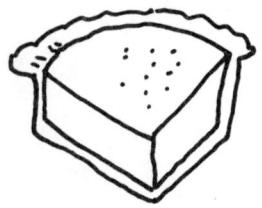

Pie Making

CHALLENGING THE HEART

Long before Little Jack Horner sat in the corner with his thumb in the Christmas pie, children have been eager to get hands-on experience in some new or forbidden activity. For Jack, you remember, it was not enough to be told the pie was good to eat. And he ignored any advice to use a fork for neatness. No, Jack dived in hands first, eager to experience plum pie with as many senses as possible.

A lot of us are like Jack. It's not enough to be told that something is good for us, or bad for us, or requires certain tools or methods for proper use. Inside us is the compelling urge to touch, taste, handle, experience things our own way.

Perhaps Thomas, Jesus' "doubting" disciple, was like that. He had trouble accepting the resurrection of Christ from the testimony of others who said, "He's alive, we've seen Him!" Instead, Thomas declared, "Unless I shall see in His hands the imprint of the nails, and put my finger into the place of the nails, and put my hand into His side, I will not believe" (John 20:25).

Later, when Jesus appeared suddenly in the room with the disciples, His first words were for Thomas. "Reach here your finger, and see My hands; and reach here your hand,

and put it into My side; and be not unbelieving, but believing" (v. 27).

Jesus pointed out that there are two kinds of learners in the world: those who need proof and those who don't. Which are you?

If you need proof, God will find a way to give it to you. Although it may not be as dramatic as Thomas' experience, God will give you "spiritual eyes" to recognize the signs around you. God does not intend for you to go through the motions of being religious. He knows that each of us needs to be convinced on a personal basis. Without that assurance, we only appear to be religious.

Prayer: God, I admit that I'm sometimes guilty of pretending I'm stronger than I really am. Inside, I have doubts about many things. I doubt myself. I doubt You. I forget You're with me and want to encourage me, that You want to help me when I am weakest.

God, give me "spiritual eyes" to see the possibilities of Your intervention in my life. Show me You're there! Amen.

CHALLENGING THE HANDS

Suggested Activities

1. If it's impractical for members to bake their own pies during the session, have the instructor demonstrate a two-crust pie assembly from scratch. Refreshments can be a pie baked during the session or brought from home.

2. An alternate idea is to have each member prepare a pie shell to take home and bake or freeze for later use.

3. Have a demonstration of ways to make different kinds of decorative edges and tops for pies: fork indentations, rope twists applied to edges, ruffle edges, chevron wedge, lattice, etc.

4. Plan to make use of your leftover dough pieces. Gather pieces and reroll to ⅛ inch thickness. Use cookie cutters to cut shapes. Prick with tines of fork. Then do any of the following (and bake at 475° for 8-10 minutes):

- Sprinkle with poppy seeds or sesame seeds, dot with butter.
- Sprinkle with cinnamon and sugar, dot with butter.
- Sprinkle with grated cheese and paprika.
- Sprinkle with garlic salt or seasoned salt.
- Cut pastry into rounds. Place small amount of jelly on one round. Top with a second round that has a hole cut in the center. Seal edges by moistening with water first.
- Cut pastry into cookie shapes. Prick, bake, cool. Spread with frosting.

If you're a novice, this chapter will initiate you into the fundamentals of truly great pie baking.

The all-important basis of a good pie is tender, flaky pastry. What is the secret? It's the way you handle the dough. Whether you choose a standard recipe or oil pastry, your success will be measured by the deft handling of the dough.

Utensils:

1. Pans can be heat-resistant glass, dull anodized aluminum, aluminum, enamel or darkened metal. Shiny metal pans reflect heat so bottom crusts are soggy. Avoid them. Pans come in 8-, 9- or 10-inch size, measured from rim to rim.

2. Pastry blender to cut shortening evenly into the flour if you are using the standard pastry recipe. You can also use two table knives in a cutting motion.

3. Pastry cloth and stockinette to ease rolling and keep pastry from sticking without picking up excess flour. You rub flour into the cloth, then roll the stockinette-covered rolling pin across the cloth to coat it lightly.

4. Rolling pin to roll the dough thin—plastic, wood, or glass. Find one that feels good.

5. Pastry wheel (optional) to cut pretty, fluted edges or make cutouts.

STANDARD PASTRY RECIPE

One-Crust Pie: For a crust on the top only (lattice or round), or for a bottom-only crust. Sometimes these are pre-baked as a shell with a no-cook filling added later.

8- or 9-inch

1 cup flour
½ teaspoon salt
⅓ cup plus 1 tablespoon shortening
2-3 tablespoons ice-cold water

10-inch

1⅓ cups flour
½ teaspoon salt
½ cup shortening
3-4 tablespoons ice-cold water

Two-Crust Pie: Great for those old-fashioned apple and berry pies. Main-dish meat pies are good, too.

8- or 9-inch

2 cups flour
1 teaspoon salt
⅔ cup plus 2 tablespoons of shortening
4-5 tablespoons ice-cold water

10-inch

2⅔ cups flour
1 teaspoon salt
1 cup shortening
7-8 tablespoons ice-cold water

Note: If you use self-rising flour, omit the salt. The flavor and texture will be different.

HOW TO MIX PASTRY DOUGH

(1)
Measure flour, salt into mixing bowl. Using an up-down chopping motion, thoroughly cut in shortening until the particles are the size of tiny peas.

(2)
Sprinkle in water, 1 tablespoon at a time. Toss with fork after each addition. (When mix is thoroughly moistened, the dough almost cleans the side of the bowl. One to two teaspoons more water can be added if necessary.)

(3)
Press dough firmly together to form a ball.

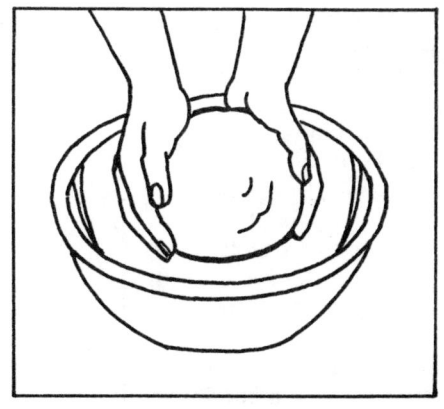

(4)
For one-crust pie, shape dough by flattening the round on a lightly floured pastry cloth or board. (For two-crust pie, divide in two pieces before rolling as above.)

(5)
With rolling pin, roll dough from the center outward. Roll evenly in all directions and be careful not to press too hard at the edges.

(6)
Keep circular shape by pushing the edge in gently with the sides of cupped hands. If any edge begins to crack, pinch it together immediately. Check to make sure the dough is not sticking to the cloth. If so, rub extra flour into cloth or working surface.
Note: If patching is necessary, moisten edge of area to be patched and press in piece of pastry.

(7)
Roll dough 2 inches larger than the diameter of inverted pie pan. Dough should be ⅛ inch thick. Use a knife to trace and cut the outline.

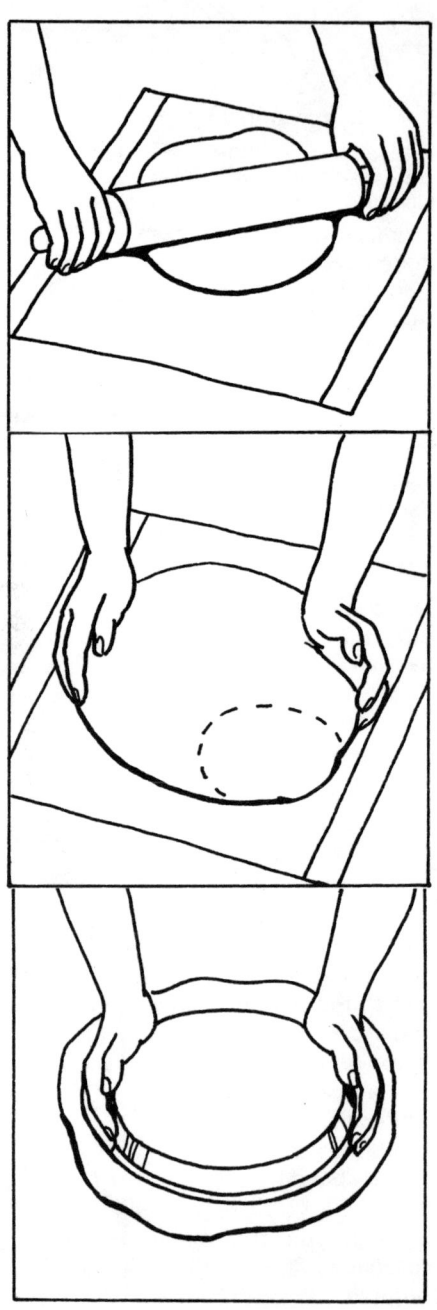

(8)
Roll pastry loosely around the rolling pin. Then unroll into the pan. This helps ensure that your circle will reach the pan in one piece.

(9)
Ease the dough gently into the pie pan and toward center by pressing with fingertips. Don't stretch! Stretching causes shrinking when baked.

(10)
Trim the edge of the dough so it extends about 1 inch beyond the rim of the pan. If you are making a two-crust pie, skip to step 12.
For a one-crust pie, fold under the dough so it is double at the rim of the pan. Pinch the edges of dough and pan together between your thumb and forefinger all around the edge to secure dough.

(11)
If your pie shell is to be pre-baked, prick the bottom and sides with a fork to prevent puffing. Bake at 475° for a metal pan or 450° for a glass pan for 8-10 minutes. Cool before filling.

(12)
If you are making a two-crust pie, roll second piece of dough 2 inches larger than inverted pie tin. Fold in quarters and cut slits along folds so steam can escape.

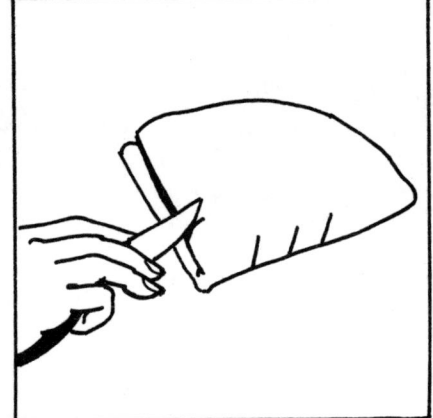

(13)
Roll loosely around rolling pin and unroll over filling. Trim overhanging edge 1 inch from rim of pan. Fold and roll the edge of top pastry under the edge of lower pastry. Press edge with fingers so it is thoroughly sealed.

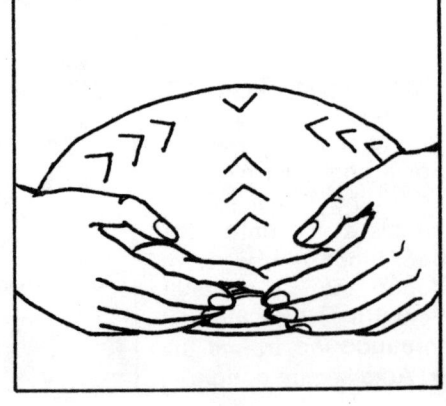

(14)
Press around pie edge with tines of a fork. Or flute by pinching the edges to form a "v" shape.

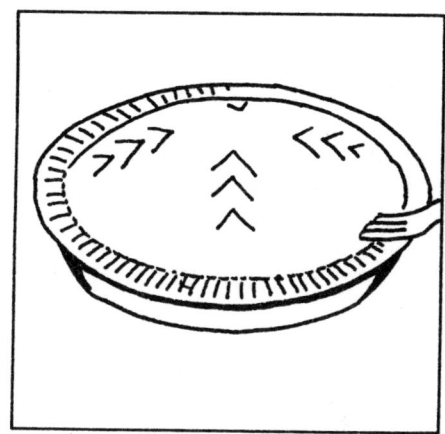

(15)
Cover edge of dough with a 2-3 inch strip of aluminum foil to prevent excessive browning. Bake as directed, except you should remove the foil during the last 15 minutes of baking.

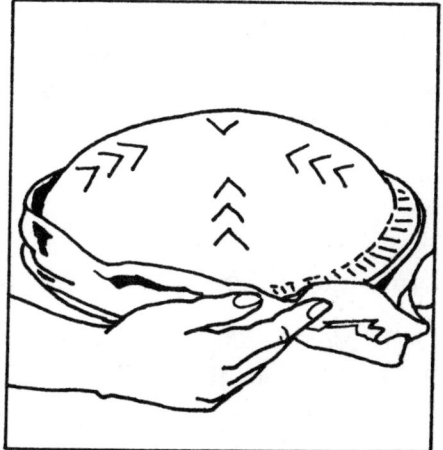

NO-COOK STRAWBERRY PIE (one-crust)

- Select the very best and loveliest of fruit. No soft spots or under-ripe sections. You will need 6 cups washed and hulled berries (1½ quarts).
- Pre-bake your pie shell.
- Mash enough berries to measure 1 cup.
- Blend 1 cup sugar with 3 tablespoons of cornstarch in saucepan.
- Add ½ cup water and mashed berries.

- Cook, stirring constantly until mixture thickens and boils.
- Boil 1 minute while stirring. Cool.
- Fill shell with remaining whole berries and pour cooked berry mixture over top.
- Refrigerate several hours.

STRAWBERRY PIE (two-crust)

- Have 4 cups of berries sliced.
- Add ½ cup of sugar, ⅓ cup flour. Mix lightly.
- Pour in unbaked pie shell.
- Sprinkle with 1 tablespoon lemon juice.
- Dot with 2 tablespoons butter.
- Add top crust (put foil on edges).
- Bake in preheated 425° oven (400° for glass pan) for 35-45 minutes, removing foil during last 15 minutes.

Make a pie without a recipe? While it is not generally recommended, in an emergency you could improvise according to the following guidelines:

1. Use 4 or more cups of fresh fruit or berries.
2. Use lemon juice for fruits that need additional tartness.
3. Lemon sprinkled over apples, pears, and peaches will prevent discoloration of fruits.
4. You'll need three more ingredients:

    Flour: ¼ to ⅓ cup
    Sugar: ⅓ to ½ cup
    Butter: 1-2 tablespoons dotted on filled pie before adding the top crust

5. Pies will need to bake at 425° (400° for glass pan), which is considered a hot rather than moderate oven.
6. Pies will need to bake anywhere from 30 to 45 minutes depending on ingredients. So keep an eye on your pies.

There is a marvelous way to have a pie that feeds a crowd, takes less time to make, and uses less crust (nice for those who are counting calories).

FAMILY PIE

- In a large saucepan, place pie crust strips around the sides of pan. If you're really counting calories, skip this and save the pastry for the top only.
- Fill with fruit lightly coated with sugar and place a hunk of butter on the top.
- Add the top crust.
- Put pie in oven at 450° to brown top of pastry. Then remove and place on the top of the stove.
- Simmer until fruit is done.

Quiche (pronounced "keesh"), a French gourmet delight, has become very popular as a meatless or low-meat dish. It's great for buffets, company, appetizers, brunches, or family dinners. Add a fresh garden salad and beverage and your meal is complete. Once you've mastered this version, think about spinach, broccoli, or mushrooms in your quiche.

QUICHE LORRAINE

(6 servings)

Pastry for 9-inch one-crust pie
12 slices (½ pound) bacon, crisply fried and crumbled
1 cup Swiss cheese (4 oz.) shredded
¼ cup minced green onion
4 eggs
2 cups whipping cream or light cream
¾ teaspoon salt, ¼ teaspoon sugar, ⅛ teaspoon cayenne pepper

- Heat oven to 425°. Prepare pastry.
- Sprinkle bacon, cheese, and onion in pastry-lined pan.
- Blend (with rotary beater) eggs, cream, and seasonings. Pour over bacon mixture.
- Bake 15 minutes.
- Reduce oven temperature to 300° and bake 30 minutes more. To test for doneness, insert knife in center. If it comes out clean without any traces of uncooked mixture clinging to blade, it's done.
- Let stand for 10 minutes before cutting.

CORNISH PASTRY

(serves 4-6)

For a meaty pie to finish up a roast and leftover vegetables, this is a crowd pleaser.

1 pound of leftover cooked meat
1 or 2 potatoes cut and diced
2 cups vegetables of your choice*
1 cup diced onion
pepper, salt, rubbed thyme
4 tablespoons butter
4 tablespoons water

*½ cup of diced turnip is barely detectable but it provides an unbelievably tasty touch

- Prepare pastry for a two-crust pie. (If you want to make individual pies, roll out dough and cut four circles ⅛ inch thick.)
- Mix the meat and vegetables together.
- Spoon into prepared pie shell, or put a generous spoonful on each individual pastry circle.
- Dot with butter and sprinkle with water. (For individual pies, 1 tablespoon butter and 1 tablespoon water for each.) Season to taste with salt, pepper and thyme.

- Moisten the edges of the pie crust with water. For large pie, place top crust and press firmly to make a seal at the edges. For individual pies, fold each circle in half to make a semicircle. Press the moistened edges firmly to create a strong seal.
- Poke with fork tines to provide escape for steam.
- Bake 1 hour at 425° (400° for glass pan).

History of Cornish Pastries: These he-man turnovers were a complete meal for even the hungriest of mine workers in Cornwall. Wives provided fresh hot pastries for their husbands each morning. The men tucked them into their shirts to keep themselves warm. Their bodies, in turn, provided heat to keep the pastries warm until lunchtime. Ingenious idea.

Recipes adapted from *Betty Crocker's Pie and Pastry Cookbook* (no longer in print), General Mills, Inc.

CHAPTER 5

Needlecrafts

CHALLENGING THE HEART

Have you ever watched ants at work? Did you press your nose close to the ground, keeping your head very still? Did you hold your breath to keep the grass from stirring?

The ants go scurrying; little legs moving swiftly in nervous bursts of energy. You put roadblocks in their paths—a test of their intelligence or persistence? Your Rocky Mountain roadblock of pebbles can't stop them. They find new ways to cope. Onward . . . forward . . . climbing . . . tunneling. They never stop.

Watch a committed needlepointer or petit pointer at work. You'll see the same persistence as nimble fingers push slender needles through tiny holes. Needleworkers are easy to spot; they tote bags full of supplies wherever they go: car rides, waiting rooms, business meetings, church. All are redeeming the time that would otherwise be spent in an aimless or unproductive manner.

Admittedly there are some who will never be skilled at needlecrafts. They will have good intentions, but unlike the worker ants, they will become distracted and forget the task they so eagerly began. When they discover the dusty reminders in drawers, they say, "Oh, I'd forgotten about this pillow I started seven years ago. Maybe one day I'll get around to completing it!" Then they close the drawer again for another seven years.

When you begin a new project, it's important to set realistic goals. Try something small for your first needlework effort. Select a piece that requires only one or two different stitches at the most. Then promise yourself this piece of needlework is going to get done! Mark a date on the calendar when you hope to have it half completed. Make use of every spare moment. Prove to yourself and those around you that you *do* have the patience and persistence to get something done.

"When the way is rough, your patience has a chance to grow. So let it grow, and don't try to squirm out of your problems. For when your patience is finally in full bloom, then you will be ready for anything, strong in character, full and complete" (James 1:3, 4, *The Living Bible*).

Think of needlework as "character work." Every stitch is reminding you of the growing character within you. And you, just like your canvas, will one day be a finished work in the eyes of God. You and God are a team working to fill in the canvas of your life, until one day you will stand before Him "complete."

Prayer: God, I want to become a patient person. I know that patience doesn't develop in the absence of difficulties and disappointments, but in the midst of them.

Whenever I must tear out or unravel a piece of my work, let me see that I must unravel faulty spots in my life as well. I must learn to pick myself up after disappointments and begin again. Give me the strength to do that. Amen.

CHALLENGING THE HANDS

It would be impossible to do justice to step-by-step procedures for learning all of the needlecrafts mentioned in this chapter. Instead, this chapter will give you some idea of the materials, possible projects and procedures for getting started. The drawings will jog your memory and serve as a handy "refresher" after you've learned the techniques. These pages are not meant to give you an in-depth coverage of needlecrafts, but rather to introduce you to new skills.

Learning any new skill will always mean some awkwardness. There will be many rows of work that must be re-done when you are a beginner. Don't be discouraged. It's part of the initiation. Your teachers will tell you of the times they had to rip out entire sections of a piece because of errors. But know that patience is the virtue that will emerge from all your persistence. Your pride and sense of accomplishment will be worth every frustrating moment.

Crochet is probably the easiest needlecraft to learn and requires the fewest accessories. It's easy to tuck in a canvas bag so you can work in spare moments while you wait for doctor's appointments or watch television.

Knitting is not difficult to learn. Learning to decipher the abbreviations used in instruction booklets is another matter! The most costly part of knitting is the expense of the yarns. A collection of different size needles will eventually be necessary.

If you're good with needle and thread, appliqué and quilting do not require the knowledge of difficult stitches that you would find in embroidery or crewel. Appliqué and quilting also make use of leftover fabrics.

Bargello and needlepoint are similar. Bargello would be the easiest and fastest for beginners to learn. Bargello technique uses larger yarns and a canvas with holes spaced farther apart. Needlepoint can be very expensive, especially if you buy ready-designed canvases.

It's possible your group may be large enough to have a demonstration of two or more crafts during your session. You might want to divide the group afterwards, allowing participants to choose the craft they prefer. Or, you may wish to divide activity time in half and allow all members to try their hand at two skills.

CROCHET

Materials: Crochet hooks and yarns may be purchased at craft shops, department or variety stores. The cost of materials is very reasonable. Look for books of patterns and instructions.

Projects:
1. Place mats are easy, since they follow a circular pattern. A chair cushion or hot pad is nice also.
2. A scarf, long or short.
3. A hat might be more difficult, but some in the class with previous experience in crochet might want to tackle it.

chair pad
hot pad
place mat

hat
scarf

EMBROIDERY

Materials: Cotton embroidery floss, needles, hoop (optional), finely woven fabrics: linens, percales, etc.

Projects: Traditionally, embroidery stitches are used on kitchen towels, hand towels, table linens, and napkins. Young girls used to monogram pillowcases and intimate apparel for their trousseaus.

Procedure:
1. Practice a few basic stitches on a sampler. Once you've mastered them, begin the project of your choice.
2. You may buy fabric already printed with designs, buy a packet of iron-on transfers, or transfer your own designs by using seamstress' chalk or tracing paper.
3. If you are a beginner, for your first project select one or two basic stitches only. (Backstitch or other outlining stitch plus a few French knots for variety are good for starters.)
4. The old-fashioned cross-stitch is another good selection for beginners.
5. Although an embroidery hoop is not mandatory, you will find that it keeps the fabric from bunching or puckering as you pull your thread through.

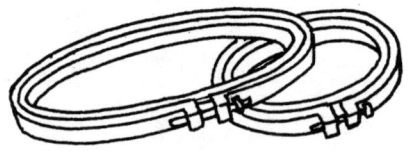

Embroidery Hoops

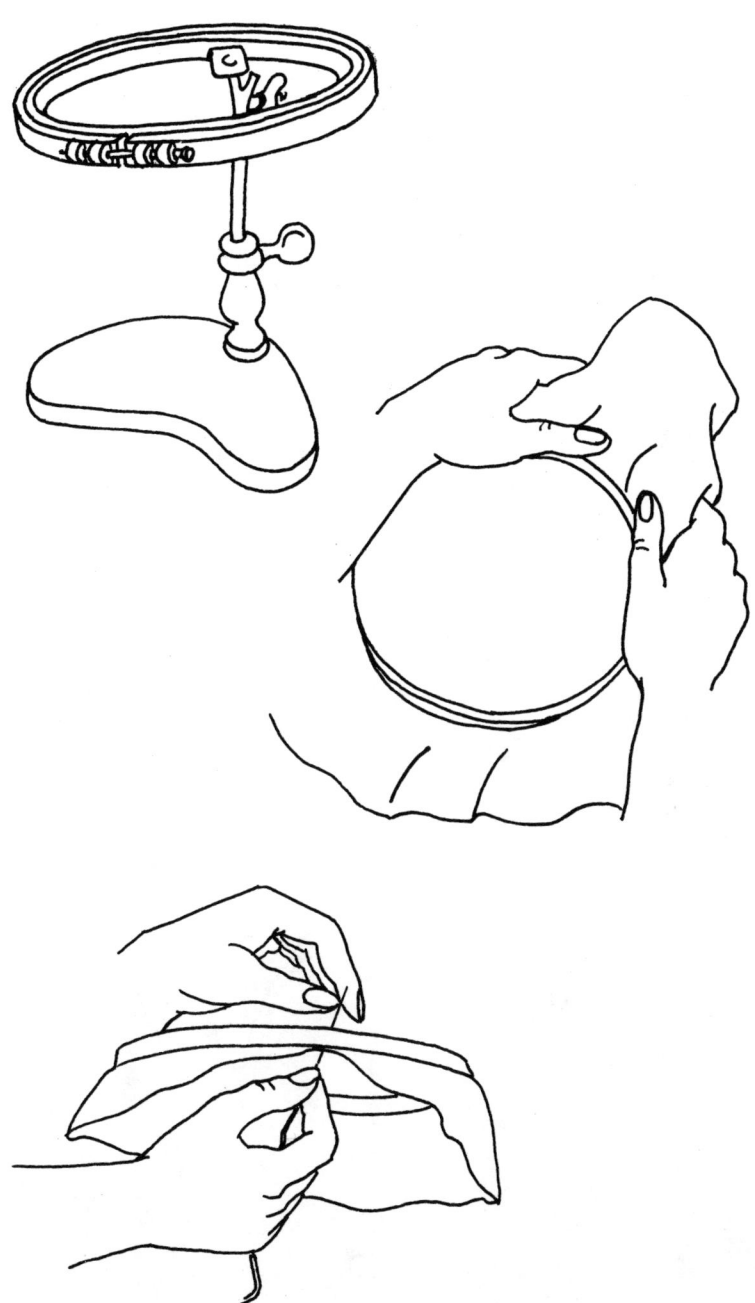

Satin Stitch

1. Come up at A.
2. Go down at B.
3. Continue to lay stitches evenly side by side. (Can be done on a slanted line as well.)

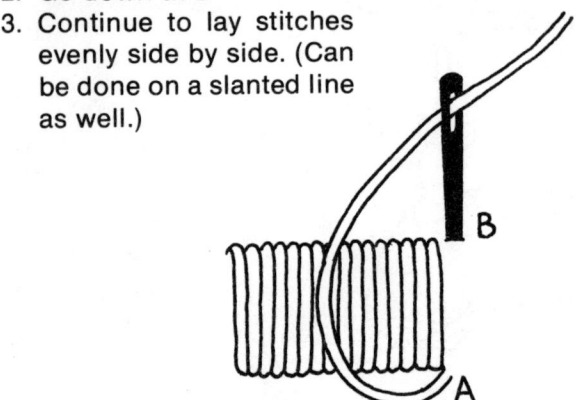

Chain Stitch

1. Bring needle up at A.
2. Form a loop and hold it down with finger as you come up at B.
3. Gently draw through and continue linking the chains.

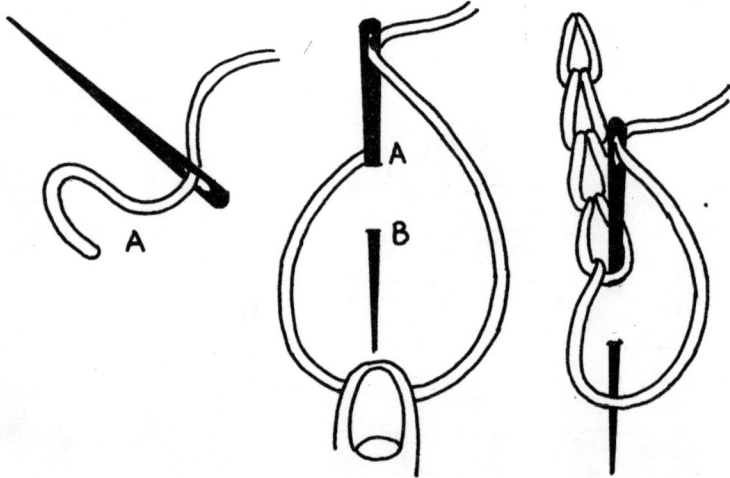

Cross Stitch*

1. Work from right to left.
2. Come up at A.
3. Go down at B.
4. Up at C.
5. Down at D.

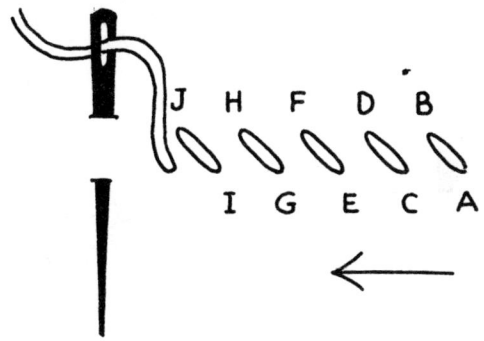

*If the needle is always kept vertical and the stitches are spaced evenly apart, the slant of each stitch will always remain the same.

6. Working from left to right, return along the line, again keeping the needle vertical.
7. Go into the exact hole of the first row of slanting stitches.

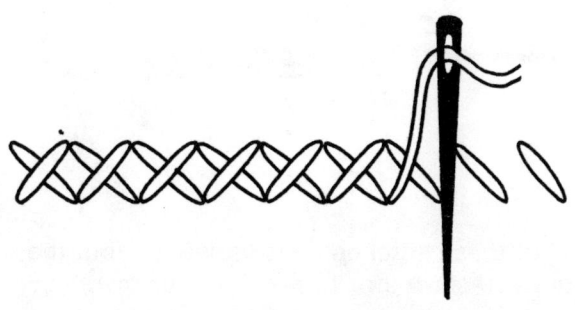

Buttonhole Stitch

1. Needle comes up at A.
2. Needle goes down at B.
3. Needle up at C (directly below B and level with A).
4. Thread is held under needle.
5. Draw through downwards.
6. Space stitches evenly.

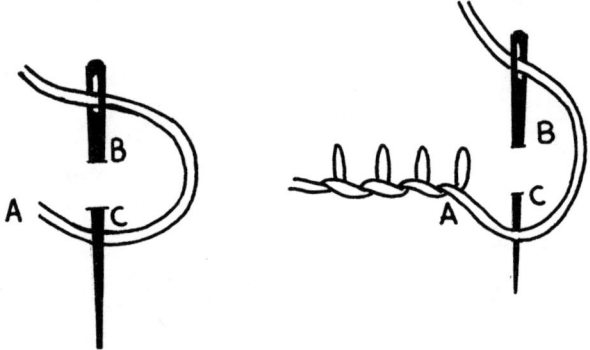

Backstitch

1. Come up at A.
2. Go down at B.
3. Come up at C.
4. Repeat, going back into same hole as the previous stitch. Keep all stitches the same size.

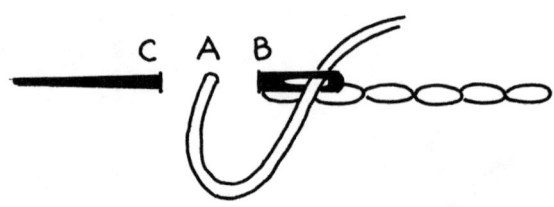

Note: All of these stitches have variations, but these are a few to get you started or to refresh your memory.

CREWEL

Crewel makes use of all the embroidery stitches and adds a few other stitches as well. With crewel, however, you have greater latitude in the kinds of fabric and yarns you may use.

Materials: crewel yarns, knitting yarns, rug yarns, linen, homespun, burlap, embroidery hoop (optional)

Projects: Pillows and decorations on clothing have become increasingly popular in recent years. Crewel can be used to make elaborate decorative wall hangings and pictures.

Procedure:
1. Learn a few stitches and make a sampler. Pick your best executed stitches to use on your project.
2. Use chalk to draw design on fabric, or purchase ready-drawn fabric kits.

Decorating with Embroidery, Crewel or Cross-Stitch

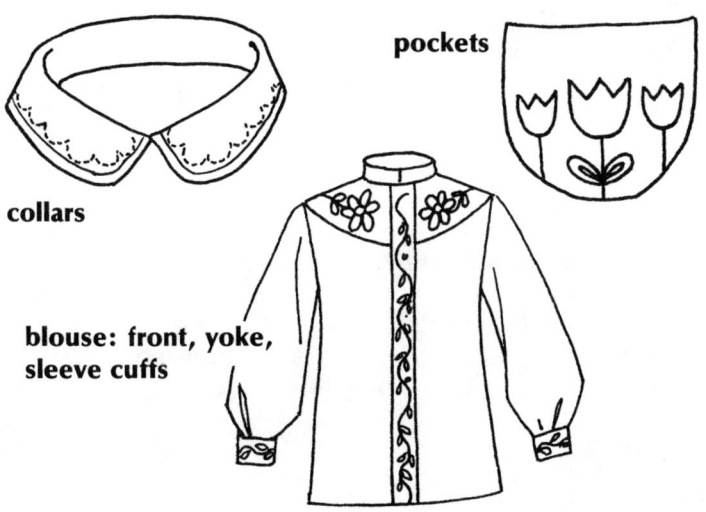

pockets

collars

blouse: front, yoke, sleeve cuffs

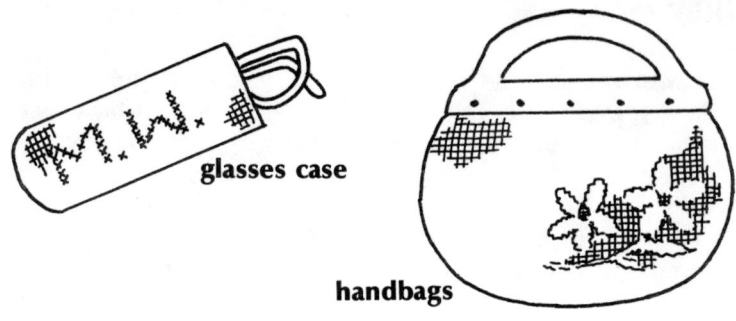

glasses case

handbags

NEEDLEPOINT

Materials: Special needlepoint canvas, plain or with printed design, needles, wool yarns, needlepoint frame (optional)
Note: Needlepoint is among the most costly of handwork crafts. Between the yarns and the canvases, it is not uncommon to spend $10-$20 on a small pillow or chair seat cover.

Projects: For beginners, bargello is like gigantic needlework. It allows you to gain a firm grasp of the concept and skill needed. Projects can be quickly completed as compared to the same size canvas with needlepoint.
Other projects might include a small picture to be framed. Pillows, glasses cases, purses, etc. are projects that will take longer.

Procedure:
1. Practice learning the continental and basket-weave stitches on a small piece of canvas. After working for several minutes, show your work to your teacher and see if she thinks you're ready to begin on a few other stitches. Make a sampler first if you wish, or select a project that requires only one stitch to keep it simple.

Types of Canvas

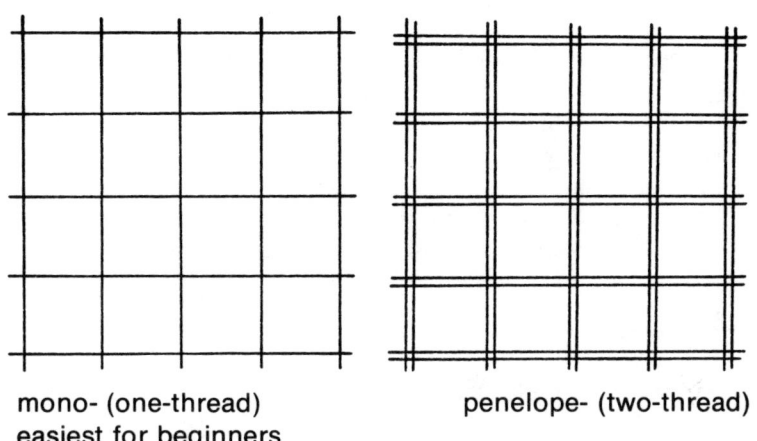

mono- (one-thread)
easiest for beginners

penelope- (two-thread)

Tent Stitch (continental)

(Gives a diagonal look on front and back.)

1. Work from left to right.
2. Work in horizontal row.
3. At end of each row, turn work upside down.
4. Work from left to right again.

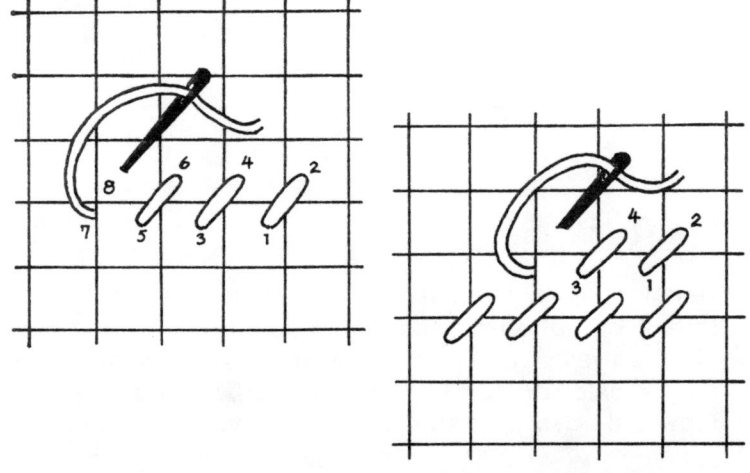

Basketweave Stitch

(also known as diagonal tent stitch)

1. More durable than the tent stitch, as the thread becomes woven into the canvas.
2. Always start in upper right corner.
3. This stitch will cause less stretch on the canvas so is better suited to hand held (rather than frame or hoop held) work. Although this stitch could be used with frame or hoop, most users like it as a "portable" stitch to use when traveling.

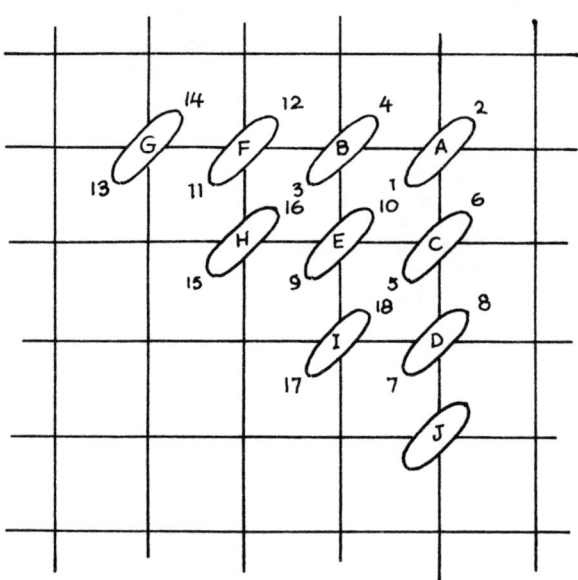

APPLIQUÉ

Materials: Sharp needles, pins, #50 mercerized cotton thread or cotton-covered polyester thread (Don't use 100% polyester!), leftover fabric scraps, broadcloth, poplin, percale, or cotton-blend fabrics, sewing machine (optional—use satin stitch, which is a very close zigzag)

Projects: Appliqué is good for so many things besides appliquéing designs to existing clothes and purses. Appliqué technique can be used on quilts. Wall hangings and pictures are very nice as well. Appliqués serve as a "first aid" to worn clothing at elbows and knees and will lengthen the life of garments.

Procedure for Hand Appliqué:

1. Cut out design one inch larger on all sides than finished size.
2. Turn under edges and press with iron.
3. On curved portions, cut a "V" wedge to allow fabric to stretch or contract as needed.
4. Secure to the background by pinning with pins ¼ inch from design edge.
5. Using a sharp needle, baste stitch ⅛ inch from design edge.
6. Now, start on backside with needle coming up through the folded edge of appliqué.
7. As you hold the fabric in your hands, fold the background fabric away from the appliqué. This looks like two folded edges on top of each other.
8. Slip in and out of each folded edge ⅛ to ¼ inches per stitch. (In other words, one stitch will go through the appliqué, the other through the fold of background fabric.)

Procedure for Machine Appliqué:

1. Complete steps 1-4 as in the instructions above.
2. Make sure securing pins are not too close to the edge of the appliqué. You don't want the machine to stitch over them.
3. If you have hand basted, the pins will not be a problem.
4. Zigzag, using a satin stitch, and remove hand basting afterwards.

Appliqué

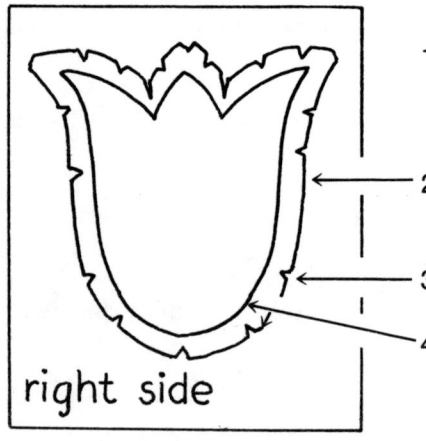

1. Trace around cardboard pattern (or draw design with tracing paper).
2. Cutting line should be 1 inch larger than design.
3. Cut "wedge" shapes on all curved edges.
4. Fold back the 1 inch margin and iron down.

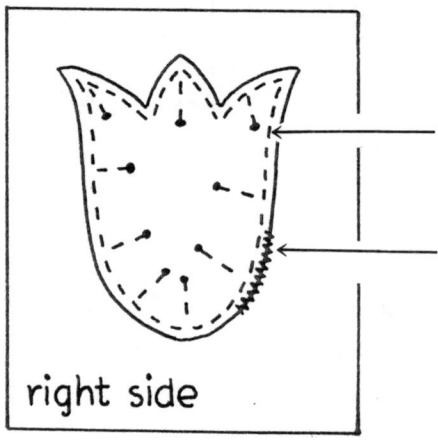

5. Pin appliqué to the right side of fabric.
6. Sew a basting stitch to hold appliqué in place, ¼ inch from edge.
7. Hand stitch or machine stitch with zigzag.
8. Remove basting stitches.

*Never use an embroidery hoop—
It stretches the fabric too much!*

QUILTING

Quilting is enjoying a revival period. Some quilts are still done completely by hand and will become tomorrow's collector's items. Others will be equally as beautiful but can be completed more quickly by sewing machine.

Materials: fabric squares or shapes for the quilted design, batting (polyester, cotton, or cotton-flannel), backing fabric for underside (crisp woven materials)

Projects: Small pillows, wall hangings, baby's quilt, quilted square to be appliquéd to purse or bib of apron, place mats.

Procedure for Beginners:
1. Two kinds of quilts are good as beginning projects. The "square to square" design uses individual squares which have been connected in long rows. Then the rows are sewn together to make a checkerboard design. A sewing machine makes it quick and easy.
2. "Crazy Quilts" are, in some respects, quicker than the orderly, evenly measured and patterned quilts. Using odd-shaped pieces of leftover fabrics, you merely turn under ¼ inch on all sides and allow the shapes to slightly overlap other pieces as you fit them together. Where the pieces overlap, you may sew by hand or machine (zigzag). When the quilt is completed, you may choose to decorate individual squares and shapes with embroidery stitches.

Turn down and press ¼ inch on edges to be overlapped on the quilt.
Overlap sections and baste in place.

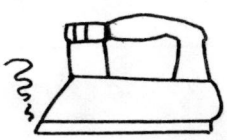

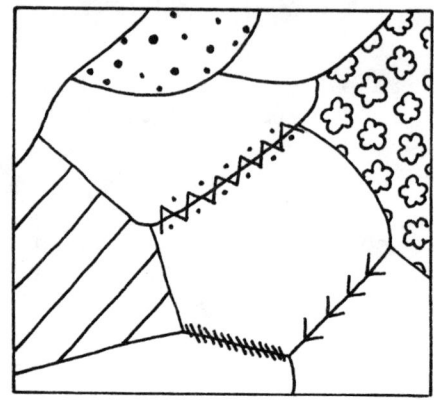

When completely covered, use embroidery or crewel stitches as finishing touch.

Sew a finished quilted square to a tote bag.

All fabrics for top layer and bottom layer should be approximately the same weight.

Batting Layer: Use preshrunk cotton batting, cotton flannel or polyester batting.

Backing Layer: Use white or off-white muslin, percale, broadcloth (cotton-polyester blends are terrific!).

"tacking" yarn

"show-off" top layer

batting layer

backing layer

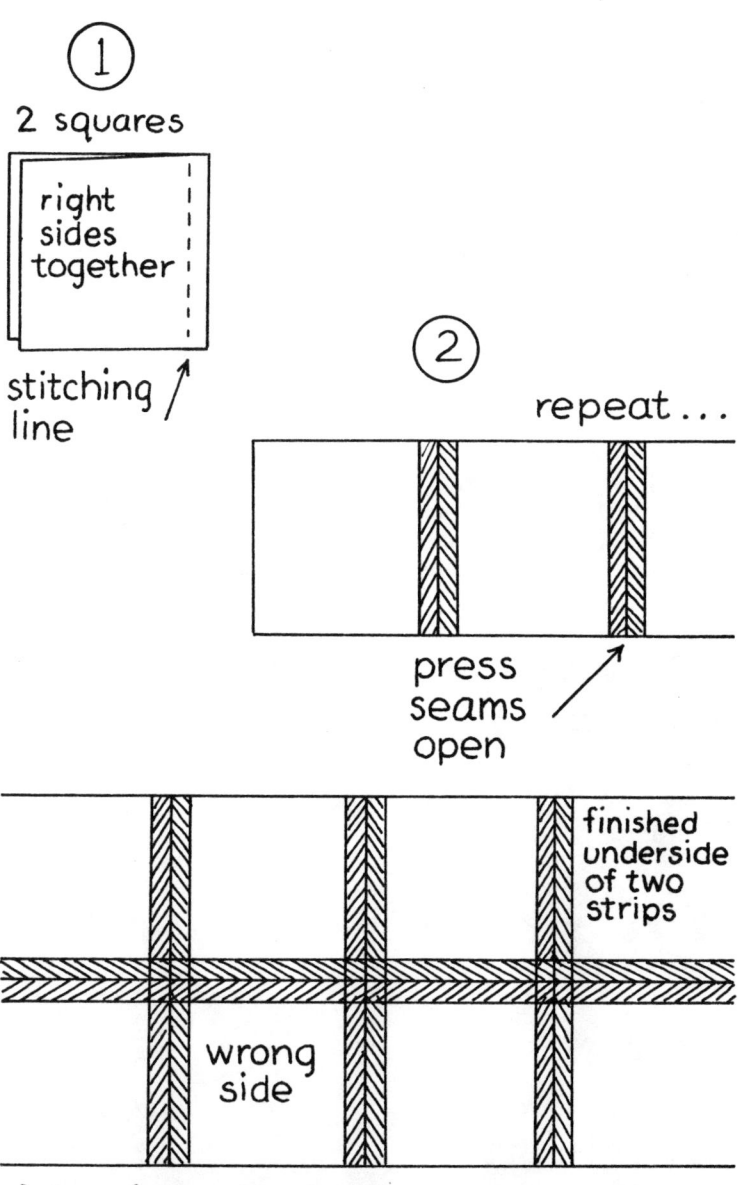

Tacking and Quilting Stitches: Used to keep the batting layer from slipping around. Yarn goes through all layers and ties in small bows.

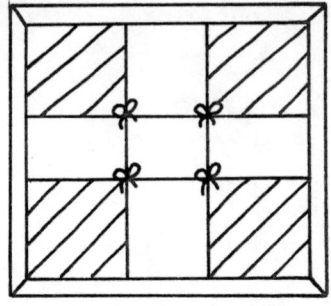

When using a quilting frame, small running stitches form designs on the quilt and also act to keep batting layers from slipping.

Binding: Using the same fabric as the backing or a contrasting color, cut bias strips and connect them. (Bias cutting allows the fabric to stretch slightly. Never use straight strips that are cut along the grain of fabric.) Your teacher will show you how to miter the corners as you bind the unfinished edges of your piece. Store-bought bias bindings can be used.

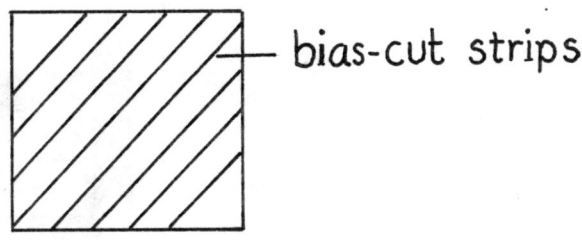

CHAPTER 6

Candle Making

CHALLENGING THE HEART

"I am the light of the world; he who follows Me shall not walk in the darkness, but shall have the light of life" (John 8:12).

In some cultures where a communal fire is a gathering point, a curious thing happens. Someone comes to carry glowing embers from the main fire to private homes. The "parent" source supplies the kindling for new fires, and soon each home has a source of its own. Should a fire die, someone from the family will be sent to a neighbor or to the main fire for another "starter" log. The fire is the main source of heat for all the community. In our devotions we are going to look at another key source—a source of strength.

Do you know where your source of strength is? To find out, ask yourself where you go when you have a problem. To a parent? A friend? A clergyman? A special place where you can be alone?

Usually, the first place we go for help is to another person. Sadly, the very best source of all, God, is often a last resort after all human help has failed.

Why? Sometimes it's pride, a little voice that says, "I shouldn't have to turn to God. I should be able to work out my problems by myself."

At other times we think, "This problem is too small for God. God handles more important matters—the big things."

God's Word says He cares about every bird that falls from the sky, and He knows every hair on your head (Matthew 10:29-31). Does that surprise you? Only a Creator who put every molecule carefully together to form mountains, mice, men, trees, butterflies, grass and the like could make a statement like that. God cares about details—the matters you and I often toss aside as insignificant.

Next time you have a problem—a serious misunderstanding with your spouse or a friend, difficulty on the job, a problem with your children—consider praying something like this.

Prayer: Lord, I want to tell You about my problem right now. (Discuss it in detail with God, just as you would with a close friend.)

Lord, if there's someone whose advice or counsel You know will help, then lead me to that person. But if I need to dwell on my problem privately and to entrust it to no one else but You, then give me the strength to remain silent. Instead, draw me to the light of Your Word. You are my source of strength. Remind me that I may need to come to You regularly for a glowing ember when my own inner fires go out. Amen.

CHALLENGING THE HANDS

SAFETY DO'S AND DON'TS

1. When melting wax, *don't melt directly over flame. Use double boiler.* Or set a trivet in a saucepan filled with water. Set the container for melting wax on top of trivet.
2. Don't leave melting wax unattended.
3. Don't heat wax to exceed 200 degrees F. Use a candy thermometer to test temperature.
4. Don't pour melted wax near an open flame.
5. Don't pour melted wax in your sink—it clogs plumbing!
6. Use plenty of old newspapers on your work area.
7. Put an aluminum pie tin under your candle mold, just in case of leakage.

IN CASE OF FIRE

1. Turn off flame. Cover pan with metal lid.
2. Don't move pan or lift lid until pan is cold to the touch. Fire may flare up again if you do.
3. Don't put water on burning wax. It spreads fire. Instead, keep box of baking soda next to work area.
4. Call fire department if you can't put fire out.

MATERIALS NEEDED

Wax

—Use large blocks available from craft shops. You will need to break it into smaller pieces.
—One 11-pound slab of wax is enough to make several medium-size candles or four quart-size candles.
—Melt down used candle remnants. Be sure you put all the same color together.

Containers for melting wax

—An old double boiler.
—An old aluminum coffee pot (never again to be used for coffee!).
—Or, use empty coffee or shortening tins. Squeeze the top lip, making a point for a spout. It makes pouring hot wax easier.
—Use a separate tin for each color you intend to make.

Heat source

—Use a gas range, electric range, or hot plate.
—Never let wax melt above 200 degrees F, or the fire hazard increases considerably. A temperature of 175 degrees is perfect. Much higher or lower than that and the candles develop peculiar pits or bubbles.
—Have a box of baking soda handy to smother flames should a flare-up occur.

Wicks

—Available at craft shops, they are sold in various thicknesses.
—Rule of thumb: small diameter candles use smaller wicks; fatter candles use thicker wicks.
—Note: The candles we will make have the wick inserted after the candle has set. It's simpler for beginners and quite satisfactory.

Molds

—For candles that will remain in the mold, you may use ceramic dishes, apothecary jars, fancy goblets or mugs, etc. For candles you wish to unmold, use glass tumblers with tall straight sides, cans, or waxed milk containers.
—Do not use plastic containers! The high heat may melt them.

Miscellaneous

—Cooking mitts that cover the hand.
—Candy thermometer to test temperature of melting wax.
—Newspaper, waxed paper, or cookie sheets to set under work area.
—Long, thin, metal knitting needles or skewers to pierce the candles and insert the wicks.
—Dye pellets may be purchased at craft store. These are added to the melted wax.
—Crayons may be used, but be careful since some have plastic additives which make candles smoke and sputter. One crayon will color one quart melted wax.

Fragrance (optional)

—Many scents are available: cinnamon, jasmine, bayberry, coconut, etc.

Now you are ready! Drop the broken chunks of wax into the melting pot or container. It will take quite a few minutes before all the wax is melted and 175 degrees is reached. (Sing or have a snack while you wait, but keep one eye on the pot at all times!) If you've decided to add color or fragrance, add them when most of the wax is melted. Stir to blend.

Now you may pour the wax into your molds. *Watch out for hot wax,* it can burn the skin. (Should you get wax on clothing, an ice cube makes it brittle enough to peel off. An ice cube applied to a burn stops the searing of the skin. Keep the ice on for at least ten minutes.)

Reserve some of the wax in the melting pot. Since wax forms an odd indentation in the middle of the candle as it cools, you'll need to refill the center. (This may have to be done twice.)

Allow the candles to cool until set before taking them home. Then let larger candles rest in their molds four or five hours before removing them. While the wax is cooling, you may want to have your devotions or refreshments.

When you're ready to add the wick, cut off a piece of wick the appropriate length, allowing an inch to extend beyond candle height. (Later it can be trimmed.) Dip the wick in hot wax to coat. Put on a mitt and hold a metal skewer or knitting needle over the flame or burner. When the needle has heated sufficiently, you can pierce a hole in the center of the candle—just large enough to insert the prepared wick. Then pour a little more wax in the center to fill up any air spaces around the wick.

Wipe spills from counters and excess wax from utensils. I've found that spraying the stove top with PAM® ahead of time makes it easy to wipe up any waxy dribbles. Leave unused wax in the melting pots. Wax can be reheated another time.

CHAPTER 7

Flower Arranging

CHALLENGING THE HEART

Can you remember exploring nature in your backyard as a young child? Did your parents show you how to smell and enjoy the fresh blossoms? Most likely you can remember using flowers as part of fantasy and pretend games. Perhaps you pretended some flowers were rare jewels as you placed them between your fingers, imagining they were gems set in rings. Perhaps you intertwined delicate posies and leaves to make garland wreaths or leis. Can you remember wearing flower crowns when you played "queen"?

If hollyhocks grew nearby, you probably made brides and bridesmaids from the blossoms. Using a big blossom turned upside down, you formed the bride's skirt. Then, with toothpicks skewered in a cross, you added a bud for the head and two buds for the arms.

A little girl asked her mother about the flowers in their garden. "Mommy," she said, "how does each one know what kind of flower it will become?"

The mother answered, "God planted a secret code in it. Even though many seeds look alike, they will not grow up alike. Some will become trees, some will be daisies, some dahlias, and so on."

You are very much like a flower. God planted a "secret code" in you, too. If you neglect or ignore some part of God's special plan for your life, you will see weeds grow up around you. The weeds will try to choke out your possibilities of becoming a mature flower.

Wouldn't it be nice to have God's entire secret plan ahead of time, like a blueprint? We all wish for that, but it is a good thing we don't have that much knowledge ahead of time.

God's plan becomes clearer the more you and Jesus grow together. When the Bible talks about being "born again," it can be compared to a seed that was planted at your birth. When you invite Jesus into your life, the seed begins to sprout. That is the starting point when all the talents you were born with take on new meaning. God wants to energize your specialness and cause "all things (to) work together for good to those who love God, to those who are called according to His purpose" (Romans 8:28).

There is another reason for allowing your growth to be gradual as your "flower" unfolds. God did not intend for you to be instantly mature. He wants you to keep returning to Him for instructions and guidelines. He uses the Bible as the "handbook" to reveal these plans. If you're lonely, you can find help in the book of Psalms. If you need to be wiser, He has provided guidelines in Proverbs and Ecclesiastes. If you're tempted to do wrong, He gives directions for overcoming temptation in 1 Corinthians 10:13.

Prayer: Thank You, God, for Your wise planning for our lives. Help us to trust You fully to reveal that plan to us in Your way and Your time. May we not neglect to read Your Word daily to feed, water, and cultivate the growth of our spirits. May the flowering of our lives bring glory to You, the Master Gardener. Amen.

CHALLENGING THE HANDS

There's something about flowers that bring out the creative and romantic aspects of a person. A roadside flower stand, flower wagons in European village squares, a garden bursting with color—all excite the eye and the sense of smell and beauty.

Perhaps you've thought only professional florists can create the appropriate mood with floral arrangements. You can, too! It's not that difficult to learn. A few simple principles and you're off on the adventure of learning how to "say it with flowers."

What will I need to get started?

Start with fresh flowers that are in season. If you use plastic or silk flowers, the same design principles will apply.

To this, add a collection of containers: low and flat, tall, round-based, square-based, formal or casual. Look around the house for unusually shaped candy jars, teapots, silver coffee servers, cream and sugar sets, and baskets. If a container is lovely but not suitable to hold water, place a smaller container inside. You will also need the following items:

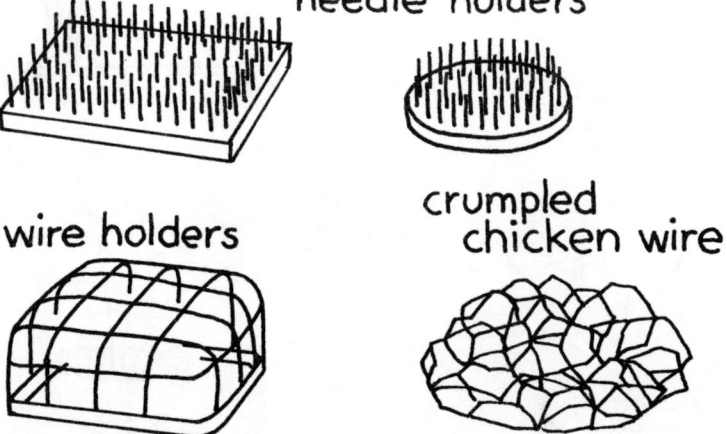

pruning shears

modeling clay

wire clippers

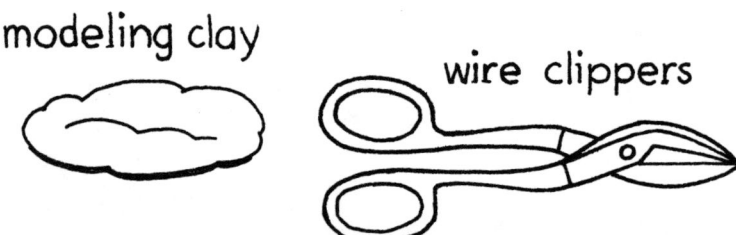

small florist wire for wayward or droopy stems

Some containers and "design lines"

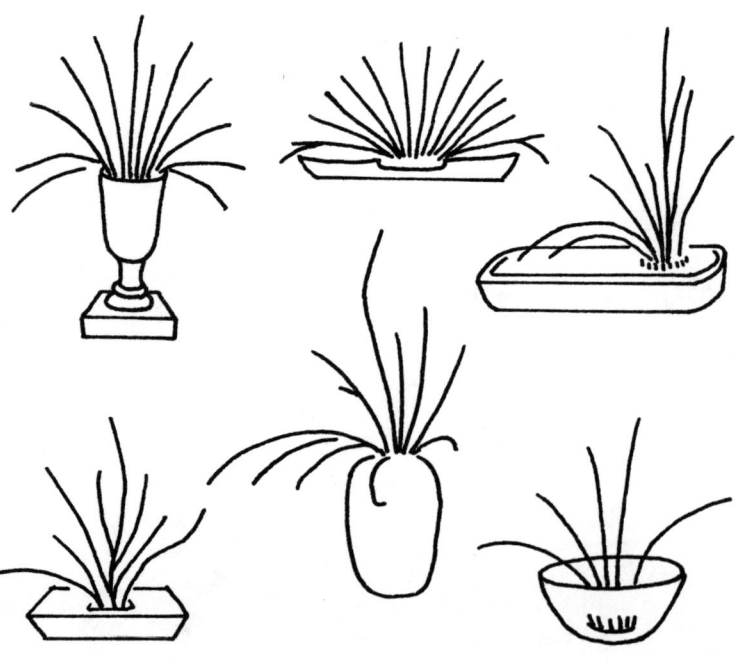

How can I keep my cut flowers fresh?

When selecting flowers from the garden, cut in the evening or early morning. Never cut flowers in the noonday heat; they droop! Plunge stems into a pail of lukewarm water as soon as they are cut. (Warm water stimulates the flow of water upwards.)

If cut flowers have been exposed to air for more than a few moments, recut the stems at an angle. This exposes more surface area and prevents air bubbles from forming on the ends of stems. Woody-stemmed flowers (chrysanthemums) and flowering branches (forsythia, fruit tree blossoms) should be crushed or split two to three inches from the bottom so they will take up more water.

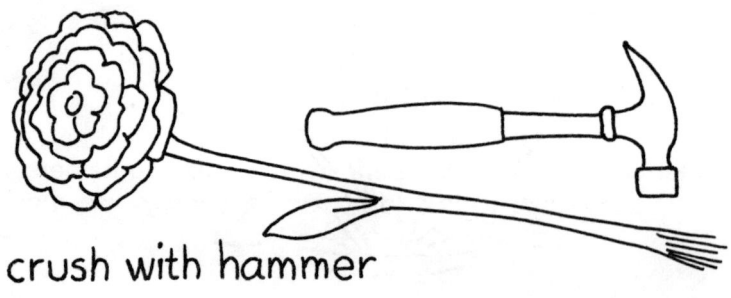

Hollow-stemmed flowers that have a milky or colorless fluid (poppies, dahlias, heliotrope) should be seared by placing the stem end in boiling water for one minute. (Alternate method: split an inch or more of the stem end. Sear over a flame.)

Change the water for your flowers every two days. To revive blooms, change water and cut about an inch off the stems. If you can't change the water add a piece of florist's charcoal. Blooms of some delicate flowers will last longer if they are misted (camellias, violets, gardenias, orchids). As a homemade flower preserver, add one teaspoon sugar to one pint of water. Or buy preserver from a florist.

Use clean containers. Bacterial growth can clog the water-conducting vessels in stems. Wash containers in warm sudsy water and a little ammonia before use. Opening of containers should be large enough that stems are not squeezed together.

DO'S AND DON'TS

Don't expose the rim of the container completely. The effect is too abrupt.

Do allow some flowers and greens to hang over the rim. It creates a smoother line.

Don't use an even number of blossoms. It's uninteresting.

Do use an odd number of blossoms: 3, 5, 7, 9, 11, etc.

Don't use flowers all the same height.

Do vary the height and size of blossoms. Use larger blossoms nearer the bottom.

Do plan on an arrangement that is 1½ to 2 times the height of your container.

Do extend the horizontal line beyond the container. Let greens and blossoms help. Double the diameter of your container to determine the total horizontal length.

Do mix a few white or offwhite colors to soften the effect. Include some very small flowers, such as baby's breath, to fill in bare spots.

Where should I start?

1. Put the tallest flower or green in the visual center first. It should be 1½ to 2 times the height of container.
2. Use a tall flower, greenery or branch horizontally to define one side.
3. Define the other side horizontally.
4. Fill in by putting flowers at varying heights halfway between one and two. Do the same for the other side. Flesh out and soften the arrangement with additional small greens, flowers or dried material.

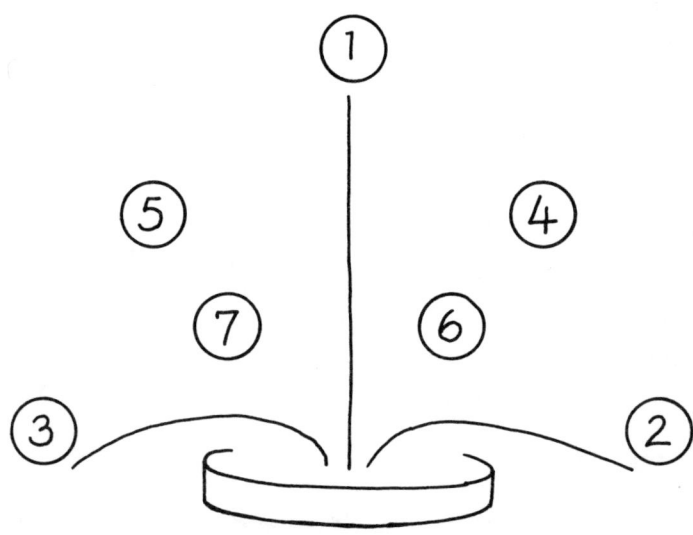

Hint: If the arrangement is to be seen from all sides, assemble it in front of a mirror. It will turn out nicely balanced!

Which color combinations work well together?

A romantic look. . . .
  blues, lavenders, greens
  lavenders and pinks
  yellow mixed with creams
  white arrangement with touch of pastel colors

A bold look. . . .
  bright colors predominate
  touch of white

A spring look. . . .
  mix the lavenders and purples (iris, bachelor buttons) with yellows (jonquil, narcissus, tulips)
  mix reds and purples or reds and blues, add a touch of daisy

Reds are exciting and festive. Yellows are uplifting and intellectually stimulating. Blues are cool and calming and will soften a formal look. Whites are formal, but they also soften the effects of other colors. Rusts, golds, bronzes, yellows create a "country" look and remind one of football games and autumn leaves. These colors appear homey and casual.

Got any other tips?

—A look in a florist shop in October and November will turn up lots of ideas for a year-round dried arrangement. Drive along a country road and you'll see lots of dried weeds that will look lovely in a basket or crockery container.

—If you choose cattails, spray them with hair spray or lacquer. Otherwise the heat from your home will cause them to puff and fly apart, creating a mess in the house.

—Although a florist has a reliable variety of greens to fill in your arrangement, you may be surprised to discover shrubs and evergreens in your own yard that are just as serviceable.

—A favorite in summer is the tall sword-like leaves of the iris. These are marvelous for giving height to an arrangement and defining the design line. Pull strands of overgrown ivy to use as the greenery in tall vases.

—Some fresh flowers will survive to be used as dried flowers. Baby's breath, often used in bridal bouquets, is a favorite. Although it is expensive to purchase, it can be used over and over.

—It's always nice to find a touch of flowers in unexpected places: on the vanity in the bathroom, beside the bed on a nightstand, a summery arrangement placed in an unused fireplace opening. Use your imagination. Maybe a single bud in a vase beside the kitchen sink will cheer you as you do your chores!

—Use a cross section of a tree trunk cut in a 1½ to 2 inch depth as a base for displaying your arrangement.

—Use brass candlesticks to flank your formal arrangement, or arrange small-scale sculpture or ceramic pieces on the table adjacent to your arrangement.

—Place a lovely tray behind your arrangement as a backdrop. Oriental or tropical fans are nice, too. If your flowers are in a teakettle or ginger jar, place the lid beside the arrangement.

—Consider making a fresh fruit or vegetable centerpiece for a surprise touch at mealtimes. Fill the container with crushed ice instead of water.

CHAPTER 8

Good Grooming and Wardrobe Selection

CHALLENGING THE HEART

"Let not your adornment be external only—braiding the hair, and wearing gold jewelry, and putting on dresses; but let it be the hidden person of the heart, with the imperishable quality of a gentle and quiet spirit, which is precious in the sight of God" (1 Peter 3:3, 4).

Through the years many have tried to legislate what a Christian should look like, an attempt that initially was meant to help a person strive for modesty. What do you think the Bible is saying about hairstyles? The wearing of jewelry? Is the Bible saying these things are sinful? No, the focus is on the motivation behind the action. A woman's behavior is what counts—her motives must be right. What she does and who she is is more important than what she wears.

What else can we learn from these verses? If we read between the lines, we'll see much more.

Beware of substituting a "modest look" as proof of your deep spirituality. You can't make yourself a Christian or guarantee salvation by going through the outward motions of looking like a Christian—however you think a Christian should look. A Christian spirit is something that comes from deep inside you. It affects the way you choose clothes, not the other way around.

Beware of substituting a "fashion look" for some character trait you are lacking. If you think fancy clothes will make up for a sharp tongue, a nasty temper, or a lack of natural physical beauty, you are sadly mistaken.

Finding who you are is often like playing hide and seek with a shadow. The "real you" is elusive. It darts about, but it is always with you. You can't escape it. It is God's job to help you find the "real you" so you can display it on the outside as well as the inside.

During the moments we spend on our hair, skin, and clothing this session, you will be learning to take care of the body that God's Word says is the "temple" where He wishes to dwell. As you look at yourself in the mirror, look beyond the nose you wish were smaller, the hair that needs a good trim, and ask yourself: "Do I spend as much time on my inner beauty (spiritual, emotional, temperamental attributes) as I do on outward beauty? And am I caring enough for my outward self that others will see I want to glorify God by the way I dress, look, and act?"

Prayer: Lord, make me hungry for those things that make me more beautiful, starting from the inside out. Make me hungry for more of You so that all the effort I put forth in making myself physically attractive will be only frosting on the cake. Amen.

CHALLENGING THE HANDS

Suggested Activities

1. Invite a hairdresser to give some tips on shampooing, haircutting, permanent waves, coloring, how to choose a flattering style, and so on.

2. Invite a makeup consultant to demonstrate good cleansing techniques and makeup application. Department stores may suggest a speaker, or you could look in the Yellow Pages to find home demonstration cosmetic companies.

3. Following the "make-it-yourself" recipes for skin care, ask members to bring the ingredients to make up some of the cleansing and facial mixtures. Let everyone try them out. Be sure to use plastic paddles or wooden popsicle sticks to dip into each recipe, since your skin chemistry may alter or contaminate the samples if you use your fingers.

4. Before your meeting, make and distribute copies of the wardrobe inventory sheet in this chapter, with instructions on how to use it, to all members. After you've discussed the wardrobe selection guidelines at your meeting, help each other analyze your wardrobes and plan needed purchases. Plan to bring your giveaway items to the next meeting to bundle them up for charity. Another follow-up idea would be to have each member wear to the next meeting her favorite daytime outfit and tell why it is flattering to her.

5. Have a "funny fashion" show with four or five girls wearing outfits that deliberately break the fashion guidelines. Divide the rest of the group into two teams. For each error spotted, that team gets one point. If time permits, make suggestions for improving each ensemble. For each suggestion, give a point. (This can also be done without using a competitive game.)

MAKEUP TIPS

Do I really need makeup?

Many women prefer to wear a bare minimum of cosmetics, perhaps just mascara, lipstick and a light moisturizer to protect the skin from direct contact with the elements (wind, smoke, pollution, sun's rays).

Others who live or work in large metropolitan centers may rely more on makeup as part of the "culture."

Moisturizers . . . Are they necessary?

A moisturizer isn't absolutely essential for very young skin, but it can prove helpful as a barrier against transmitting soil and bacteria to the skin's pores from touching the face. Most people touch their face frequently during the day and do so unconsciously.

If you are over twenty-five, your skin is beginning to reverse the process from growing up to growing old. Of course, you can't see this process beginning unless you have a powerful microscope. But it's happening, just the same. Also, you'll find that if you use a foundation, the makeup can be mixed with small amounts of moisturizer or the moisturizers can be used before applying the foundation. In either case, the foundation will slip on so much better.

How do you apply foundation?

The professionals use a damp but almost dry sponge. They say it goes on easier, more evenly, and doesn't use as much makeup.

If you're using the correct foundation color, you should have very little "line" to show where you stopped application. Using the sponge applicator, you can "feather" your finish line and no one will know.

Your skin's pores aim downward. For even coverage, work upward in sweeping movements toward the temples. On the forehead move from the center outward. Don't pull downward. Gravity is doing all it can to speed up the sagging and aging process, so don't cooperate!

Never use your index finger to apply makeup. It exerts more tissue-pulling pressure than any other finger. Use your middle finger.

Eye tissue is very delicate. The skin layers are so thin that once damaged, they cannot be restored easily. If you're over thirty you should be using a lubricating eye cream at night. Start at the outer corners of the eye, using that middle finger, and aim toward the corner of the eye near the nose. If you wait until the wrinkles show, it's too late!

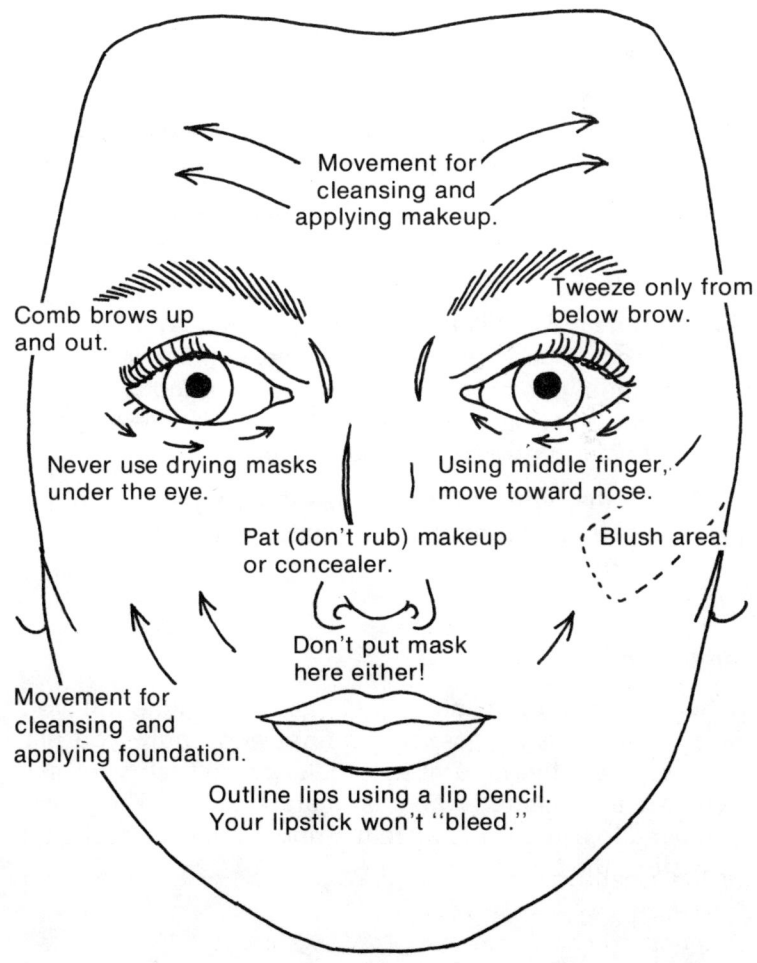

BASIC SKIN CARE

From materials you would find around the house, and with a visit to your pharmacist and produce vendor, you can whip up batches of your own penny-wise cosmetics. Many of the recipes that follow were used before business enterprises got into the cosmetic field. See if your grandmother can remember more home remedies and recipes to share with you.

First, though, you need to know your skin type.

Dry Skin: Patches of dryness. Itchy skin during winter months.

Oily Skin: Characteristic shiny patches around the nose, chin, and forehead which appear even a few hours after cleansing or applying makeup. Large pores. Oily hair.

Combination Skin: If you have a combination normal/dry skin, follow directions for dry skin. If your skin is normal/oily, follow directions for oily skin.

Acne: Acne can afflict any skin type. It may be due to hormonal changes during adolescence, infrequent shampooing, improper daily cleansing, infection or skin disease. A dermatologist is the best person to diagnose any special problems you may have.

Choose the right kind of cleanser for your skin type. The right selection ensures that the natural acid state will return to your skin.

Isn't plain soap best?

Soap is mainly alkaline (acid-neutral). Although your face "feels" clean because it's tight and tingly, you may have stripped the natural acid balance and left your skin vulnerable to bacteria and premature aging. That's why you need to use an acid rinse (astringent or skin freshener) to restore the balance.

How often should I cleanse my face?

In the morning, use the cleanser appropriate for your skin type. Follow with an astringent. Apply moisturizer (if you're over twenty-five especially). Then apply foundation if you use one.

In the evening you must work doubly hard. Cleanse twice and use astringent twice. You've been in air that may be polluted by smog and other irritants. You've perspired. You need to get your makeup off. So wash, rinse, astringent and repeat! Now you're really clean. (This is the best remedy for blackheads. They don't have a chance to form!)

What temperature water should I use to rinse my face?

Some advise very warm or lukewarm water in the beginning with a final cold rinse to close the pores. Nona Aguilar, author of *Totally Natural Beauty,* believes very warm water allows the natural secretions to flow outward to bathe the complexion. She also points out that blood capillaries expand to allow a freer flow of blood for circulation. If your skin is oily, she says, you should use water as warm as possible.

BASIC OATMEAL SCRUB

½ cup oatmeal (uncooked) ground in blender until a fine powder

1. Splash face with warm water.
2. Apply oatmeal powder with moist fingers.
3. Rub gently over entire face.
4. Rinse with lots of warm water.
5. Repeat above using 15 splashes of rinse at end.

BASIC ASTRINGENT

⅛ cup vinegar
1½ cups water

1. Combine and store in jar or bottle.
2. Apply with water-moistened cotton ball. (If your face stings, you forgot to moisten the cotton ball with water first!)
3. Let your face air dry unless you have dry skin.

My skin needs deep cleansing. What should I use?

Because skin is an organ for excreting body wastes, a deep cleansing should be done at least once a week for those with normal skin. Oily skin may require more.

OILY DEEP CLEANSER

1 cup oatmeal (blend till flaky, not powdered)
¼ cup farina (available in cereal section of grocery)
1 tablespoon salt

Apply to skin same as other cleansers. This cleanser is a good scrubber and provides some abrasive action.

DRY DEEP CLEANSER

1 cup oatmeal (blend till flaky)
1 tablespoon farina

Use this if your skin tends toward dryness or if your skin is sensitive.

What can I use for blackheads?

For oily skin, rub 1 teaspoon of yogurt on face. Rinse after a few minutes. Mix 1 heaping tablespoon baking soda with 1 tablespoon water. Rub gently on skin for 2-3 minutes. Rinse with 30-40 splashes of very warm water. Follow with astringent or vinegar rinse.

For sensitive skin, mix 2 tablespoons heated honey with 2 tablespoons untoasted wheat germ. Rub on face for 3-4 minutes. Then leave on face for 15-20 minutes. Rinse with 30-40 splashes of very warm water and follow with a vinegar rinse.

What about masks?

A mask is left on the face to condition or tighten, and in some cases is used to pull off dead debris that is clinging to the skin.

Some believe that a mask should still let the skin breathe and should remain soft rather than forming a dry peel-away film. Others recommend the peel-away mask because of the rush of circulation to the skin's surface when the mask is removed. Try both and see which one you like best.

For Dry Skin

AVOCADO MASK

Peel and mash an avocado. Spread over face. Leave on for a few minutes then rinse off with plenty of splashes.

EGG WHITE MASK

Whip egg whites until frothy. Apply with fingertips. Allow to dry until glistening and shiny. Wash off with warm water.

MAYONNAISE MASK

4 teaspoons mayonnaise
1 teaspoon fuller's earth (powdered clay from the pharmacy)
1 egg yolk
Have on hand a measuring spoon, bowl and 2 thick brushes

Mix mayonnaise and fuller's earth to form a paste. If your skin has lots of lines or is very dry, brush a layer of pure egg yolk on your face BEFORE applying the mask. Otherwise spread the paste directly on skin. Leave on 10 minutes. Rinse with tepid water.

For Oily Skin

HONEY-MINT-YOGURT MASK

1 teaspoon honey
½ cup plain yogurt
1 tablespoon fuller's earth
2 drops mint extract
1 pinch bicarbonate of soda

Mix the above and apply to face with a brush. Yogurt softens the skin while the fuller's earth and honey will pull surface impurities from it.

Apply dampened strips of cotton (surgical roll) to face "mummy" fashion, leaving holes for eyes, nostrils, and lips. Rest for 10 minutes. Remove cotton. Rinse off mask.

Facial recipes from *Totally Natural Beauty* by Nona Aguilar (out of print), Rawson Associates.

HAIR CARE

How often should I have my hair cut or trimmed?

Hair grows about one-quarter inch per month. To keep uneven growth from giving hair a shapeless, shaggy look, it's good to have it trimmed every four to six weeks. Even if you're trying to let your hair grow out, the trim keeps your hair tidy.

Do I need conditioners?

There are many things that make for troubled hair: sun, wind, smog, air pollutants, poor diet, medications, and perhaps a host of other as yet unknown sources. By paying attention to regular preventive measures, you can avoid many problems. Wear a head covering in the sun. Use a hair spray that contains sunscreen or conditioners.

Improve your diet. Don't over-dry the ends of your hair with a blow dryer; aim the dryer at the root ends.

Coloring, bleaching, tinting and permanent wave lotions can rob hair of essential oils and elasticity. It's best to follow these treatments with a good conditioner. For an at-home conditioning treatment you could try the following.

OIL TREATMENT

1. Heat olive oil in a saucepan.
2. Apply to hair with fingers or brush.
3. Massage well into hair.
4. Apply a hot towel. (Soak towel in very hot water. Wring out.)
5. Leave on head for 15-20 minutes.
6. Shampoo and set or blow dry.

MAYONNAISE PACK

1. Rub mayonnaise into the hair. The egg and oil combination makes a good conditioner.
2. Leave on hair for 15-20 minutes.
3. You may use the hot towel treatment if you wish.
4. Shampoo.

WARDROBE SELECTION

Suppose your life-style were to be changed drastically and you had to trim your wardrobe to only the barest of essentials. What would you choose? Here are some helpful guidelines to ensure your minimum wardrobe will be balanced.

1 coat (A bright color will cheer you on a wintry day.)
1 matching skirt in the same color as the coat
1 sweater in a complementary color
1 dark, solid-color skirt
2 blouses

2 cotton shirts (for summer)
2 pair of shoes
1 pair of sandals (summer)
2 pair of slacks
1 pair of shorts
2 wool sweaters
1 black or dark handbag (winter)
1 straw or fabric handbag (summer)
1 pearl necklace or simple chain

In case you're thinking this wardrobe is skimpy, remember that most of us prefer the same four or five outfits, even if our closet is full of clothes.

Clothing Tips

—Sit down in your clothes before you buy them.

—Matching accessories are best when paired:
　　hat—gloves
　　bag—shoes
　　hat—bag
　　shoes—gloves

—To make the hemline of coats or evening gowns hang like expensive designer clothes, run lightweight chain inside the hem.

—If you sew suits or coats (or if you buy them), make sure you ask the cleaners to give you a "rolled" neckline and collar or lapel pressing. Otherwise your expensive-looking garment will develop a permanent crease.

—"Be not too early in fashion, nor too long out of it; nor at any time in the extremes of it" (LaVater). High fashion points toward trends by overemphasizing. If broad collars are in, for example, choose a garment that is not quite as broad, but still in keeping with the "trend."

—Hairstyles should complement the wardrobe, not compete with it. Find a flattering hairstyle and work with variations of it.

Colors That Complement

For pastel colors as the main ensemble . . .
 white—black or bright hues
 pink—beige, purple, mauve, navy, gray
 beige—black, brown, red, green
 gray—brown, dark green, dark gray, red

If your basic color is dark . . .
 black—beige, white, toast, yellow (avoid pastels of pink or blue)
 navy—white, lemon yellow, raspberry, bright green, mauve
 red—black, blue or navy blue
 brown—white, beige, black, orange-red, red, orange, dark green
 plum—sky blue
 dark red—black, sky blue, beige

Don't trust your "favorite color" theory. Often the colors you like will not be those that best complement your skin tones.

Instead, you might like to enlist the help of a few friends. What colors have brought you the most compliments—pastels, earth tones, bright splashy colors, sophisticated blacks or crisp whites?

Color affects not only how we feel about ourselves, but how others respond to us. Bright, bold colors suggest, "I am in charge." Pastel colors tend to make others want to get close to us—they're nonthreatening tones. Classic lines and sharp contrasts in color may suggest, "I'm a professional."

Some communities have colorists or color consultants who are trained to help you find your "right" colors. Their expertise will help you avoid costly mistakes, and you'll be able to beeline toward "your colors" on the clothing racks. This will save you both time and money for the rest of your clothes-buying days. Such advice is not cheap, however.

There are other ways of developing a color sense. Take a friend or two with you next time you shop. Go to the racks and select a garment with an eye for style only. (Most people select color first.) Hold up every color combination in that style. Stand in front of a mirror and look at yourself. You may be surprised that some of the colors that did not initially appeal to you are actually quite flattering. Which colors make your complexion radiate and glow? Which colors drain color from the face?

Ask your friends to score each color from 1 to 10. Forget about those colors and hues that receive a 5-7 score or below. Concentrate on those colors that really say something!

Do's and Don'ts for Your Figure Type

"Hourglass" figure, well proportioned

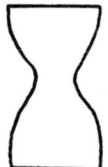

A typical "hourglass" would be tall, 5'8" or so and weigh no more than 120 pounds.

AVOID	ENJOY
extremely high heels	narrow skirts
vertical stripes	long hair
	slacks
	enormous cloaks
	wide collars
	big hats
	the "latest" in fashion

"Top-heavy" figure

A typical "top-heavy" would be full-figured or endowed with a generous bust. The lower part of the body is slender. It is probably easier to list what she should wear, rather than clothes to avoid.

ENJOY

V-necklines
dresses that button down the front
single-breasted coats and suits
draped bodices
straight skirts
straight coats (could be tapered at the hem)
tailored suits with collars and lapels
crepe and other soft materials
large toques or wide-brimmed hats
slacks with unfitted blouses

Hide what is too generous; accentuate the slimmest part of the figure.

The "oval"
(plump, pleasingly or otherwise)

A typical "oval" type might be 5'3" and weigh around 128 pounds with a larger waist in proportion to the hips.

AVOID	ENJOY
narrow skirts	A-line dresses and skirts
clinging sheaths	slightly flared hemlines
wide-shouldered coats	nonclingy wools
large collars	bateau or high round necklines
big hats	pleated, gored, and full skirts
horizontal stripes	high Empire waistlines
shift dresses	coats, coatdresses, capes
shawls with short skirts	scarves, stoles
flat shoes with narrow skirts	vertical lines
tunics	long, rather full-skirted dresses
short, stiff peplums	
floating chiffon dresses	
giant prints	
shiny satins	

"Bottom-heavy" figure

This is similar to the average plump woman (or even the expectant mother).

ENJOY

Empire and Trapeze styles
scarves, collars, etc. to attract eye upward
vertical lines
A-line dresses and skirts
slightly flared hemlines
high round necklines
bateau necklines
nonclingy fabrics

Again, emphasize your best feature and downplay the hip area.

WARDROBE INVENTORY CHART

Article	Condition			Color Family								Needs Replacing	Additional Needs
	Ex.	Good	Ugh!	R	Wh	Blu	Grn	Y	Brn	Or	Blk	Other	Estimated cost Where to buy	Estimated cost Where to buy
													(Use this during "Finance" session.)	

How to Use the Wardrobe Chart

1. Get a friend to help you.

2. Take all your clothes out of the closet. Group them according to the following categories (add others if you need to):

    Coats   Sweaters
    Dresses   Jackets
    Skirts   Belts
    Blouses   Hats
    Pants   Shoes
    Suits and ensembles   Gloves

3. Pick one category. While your friend writes down the entries in pencil, you hold up each garment and decide: Is it in excellent condition, good condition, or poor condition? Put a check mark in the appropriate column.

4. Now have your friend record the color family for each garment: Rd=Red, Wh=White, Blu=Blue, Grn=Green, Y=Yellow, Brn=Brown, Or=Orange, Blk=Black. (Continue adding other colors like Pink, Gray, Tan, Gold, Purple, Lavender, etc. If you come to a plaid, pick out the predominant color.)

5. If you see that some garments don't have anything that goes with them (i.e., yellow plaid skirt but no harmonizing sweater or blouse), record at the far right of your chart, under the heading "Additional Needs," "Buy yellow sweater." Later you can go to the store and price articles, but for now, all you want to do is make a record.

6. If any article is showing signs of fading, fraying, or other signs of age, make a note under "Needs Replacing" to replace that article. But make sure it's an article that you'd use with frequency or one that is necessary to complete an ensemble. If you don't plan to replace it (perhaps it's out-of-date or style), toss it in a giveaway pile.

7. If you come to an article you haven't used in two years, ask yourself, "Is it because I don't have anything to

go with it? Even if I found something to go with it, would I really wear it?" If you haven't used something in two years, the odds are against your ever wearing it again; so you might as well put it in the giveaway pile.

8. Now that you've eliminated the giveaways, look at what's left. Which items are your favorites? Lay aside those articles. If any article (say a pair of slacks) needs an accompanying blouse or sweater, did you remember to record it under the "Additional Needs" column? Pay close attention to your recommendations for color.

9. Look at your "Needs Replacing" and "Additional Needs" lists. Your lists should easily cover those items needed to make your wardrobe complete. When you go shopping, take the lists with you so you won't be sidetracked into buying extras.

10. Here's an idea to help you move from season to season in style. Pick two or at the most three colors to be the mainstays in your wardrobe. For example, tan and red might be main colors for summer. When you move into fall and winter, add black. Look for items that will go well with red or black. For spring, think about red and blue. You're all set to add white for the summer season so that red and blue blouses, for example, will have a crisp accompaniment. By doing this, you'll have a closet full of clothes you'll use regularly. Pick your main colors before you go shopping so you won't get sidetracked.

11. Finally, go window shopping with your friends. In the last two columns record the place and the price where you saw an item you needed. Then go back over your list and zero in on the best buy. If you ever needed data to convince yourself of necessary expenditures, now you've got it. No ill-defined, "I think I need a new blouse." Now you've got a sensibly laid out plan with prices and places. Your budget can be planned and altered with wisdom. Congratulations! You've graduated from being an impulse buyer to an informed shopper.

12. Bundle up your giveaway pile and take it to a secondhand clothing shop or send it to a mission or charity.

Excerpts from ELEGANCE by Genevieve Antoine Dariaux. Copyright © 1964 by Genevieve Antoine Dariaux. Reprinted by permission of Doubleday & Company, Inc.

CHAPTER 9

Money Management

CHALLENGING THE HEART

"We have brought nothing into the world, so we cannot take anything out of it either. And if we have food and covering, with these we shall be content. . . . For the love of money is a root of all sorts of evil, and some by longing for it have wandered away from the faith, and pierced themselves with many a pang" (1 Timothy 6:7, 8, 10).

"Where your treasure is, there will your heart be also" (Matthew 6:21).

There is a story about a young Japanese exchange student who was a Christian. One day an acquaintance, who was not a Christian, said to him, "Yurio, I've been watching you. You seem to me like someone who must have a very wealthy father."

"Why do you say that?" Yurio wanted to know.

"Because you are always smiling, you seem happy and you never worry much. Your father must have given you much for you to have so few problems in life."

There was something about Yurio that the acquaintance did not know. When Yurio became a Christian, his father cut him off from the family because he had left the religion of his ancestors.

Yurio did have a rich father—but it was his heavenly Father. That heavenly Father had given him something that his new friend had mistakenly assumed was material wealth. So the Japanese boy said, "If it had not been for the riches of my heavenly Father—His mercy and kindness toward me—it would have been impossible for me to have endured the loneliness I have suffered since being cut off from my relatives."

Does that mean that everyone who becomes a Christian must lose loved ones and friends? No. Sometimes it happens, but when a relationship is lost, God is able to replace the emptiness with a most unusual, unexplainable peace.

Does being a Christian mean I have to give up things I hold dear? Do I have to live a life of poverty and cease to enjoy beautiful things? No. The Bible says, "The love of money is a root of all sorts of evil." It does not say that money or material blessings by themselves are evil. In fact, some Christians have been placed in positions of great wealth and abundance by God himself. It is your motives and goals that are important: How important is material wealth to you? Why do you desire it? How will you acquire it? How will you use it?

If you reach for God's best in your life, if your sole purpose for living is to give Him honor in all you do, then whatever blessings He gives you will seem like an overflowing cup of goodness. Should you be blessed with little or much, either way you'll feel "rich."

Prayer: Lord, help me see that I never truly get a handle on my finances and my life if I give You only the "leftovers." If I give You what's left of my allowance, if I give You time in my life only when it's convenient for me, if I read my Bible only when I've finished everything else I have to do first—those things are leftovers.

Forgive me for the times I wanted something so badly that I didn't want to hear You or anyone else say, "This is not right for you." As I spend this time thinking about my possessions, remind me that all I have is on loan from You during my stay on earth. Make me open to possibilities for using my money and my time to do greater good for others instead of doing only those things that satisfy me first. Amen.

CHALLENGING THE HANDS

Suggested Activities

1. Give a "shrewd shoppers" award for the one who made the best purchases using the wardrobe chart in the previous "Grooming and Wardrobe" chapter. Judge by how well she analyzed her wardrobe needs, her thoroughness in checking stores, and the appropriateness of her purchases.

2. Make an organizer for the pay-your-bills notebook described in this chapter. Bring in all your charge slips and bills and organize your notebook in class. Provide felt-tip pens or neat labels for a professional touch.

3. This chapter assumes that your members are following some sort of basic budget plan already. It consists mainly of practical tips for controlling impulse buying, setting saving goals, managing credit buying, and so on. If your members indicate a need for basic budgeting know-how, invite a speaker to address this topic before you discuss the tips in this chapter.

SMART BUYING HABITS

Some people naturally have a keen sense of wisdom in making money-related decisions. Others flounder through math courses, flunk check-balancing exercises, and are perpetual victims of impulse buying. Where do you stand?

—Do you have a hard time telling a salesperson "no"?
—Do you often buy more than you intended?
—Do you buy something you think you can't live without, only to discover that it sits idle much of the time?
—Do you have a policy of always buying the cheapest item?

If you answered "yes" to any of the above, this session has something in it for you.

All of the following suggestions are geared to the person who is not a whiz with numbers. For those of us with weak money sense, there are ways to help us keep ourselves from going bankrupt, or putting an unnecessary strain on family relationships. (Statistics show that the greatest problems in marriage stem from money-related matters.) These techniques and guidelines are not hard to learn.

If you know your sales resistance is weak, stop patronizing those stores whose products constantly keep your budget in turmoil. When a salesperson starts pressuring you to buy, here are some answers to help you say "no."

- "I haven't made up my mind yet."
- "This is my first stop in comparison shopping, and it's my policy never to buy the first item I see."
- "Your product is lovely, but it isn't a high-priority item at this time. Thank you for your helpfulness."
- "I want to bring my husband to see this before I make the final decision."
- "I can't put this on my credit card—I've reached my limit."

Don't succumb to another sales pitch: "Would you like to apply for one of our charge accounts?" Limit yourself to two active charge accounts, and tell the salesperson that is your rule. Don't habitually charge small items.

While it may be necessary to make use of charges for large purchases, appliances, etc., it is not a good idea to charge things that have a short life expectancy. Don't go into debt for something that will be "consumed" before you've paid for it. If you must charge clothes at the beginning of a school year, promise yourself that all other such purchases will be strictly on a cash basis for the remainder of the year. You might want to consider layaway options instead of immediate purchase.

Use a charge account as a last resort, not a first impulse. By saying, "Oh we can always charge it," you are setting yourself up for debt problems.

Shopper's Store Guide

Department Store

Variety of nationally advertised merchandise. Sells at full retail except for sales.

Discounts: 10%-30% off when item is on sale.
Pluses: Can return or exchange items. Charge and layaway.
Minuses: Merchandise discounted only during sale periods.

Chain Store

One of a group of stores. Less expensive and/or copies of more expensive items are available.

Discounts: Sale items usually discounted 10%.
Pluses: Can return exchanges to any other store in the same chain.

Boutique

Small specialty store. Usually a single line such as women's clothing and accessories.

Discounts: 10%-50% only when an item is on sale.
Pluses: One-of-a-kind goods. May have altering services.
Minuses: Regular prices are 200% over wholesale.

Discount Store

Regularly sells merchandise at discounted prices.

Discounts: 20%-40%
Pluses: Can buy nationally advertised merchandise at discount prices anytime. Will "special order" on request.
Minuses: May have to wait for items to be ordered. Often has limited return policy.

Factory Outlet

A clothing outlet that makes a garment and then sells it wholesale.

Discounts: 35% to 50%
Pluses: Quality merchandise at low prices. Occasionally "seconds" or "irregulars" with minor flaws.
Minuses: May require cash only. No sales assistance.

Secondhand Store

Used clothing that has been donated or is sold on consignment.

Discounts: Clothes at a fraction of the original cost.
Pluses: Some very chic and fashionable ladies give their clothes to such stores. Designer clothes for a fraction.
Minuses: Not all stores carry top-line garments. Some will have rummage-sale quality. Must shop frequently to find the real bargains.

You can see that when a top-line store or specialty shop has a sale, you may end up with superior quality at up to 50% savings. Some people plan their purchases to take advantage of those sales. (Call the store to find out their dates for big sales.) It is possible to actually come out farther ahead this way than if you shopped only the discount and factory outlets. A truly well-made garment will last you years longer than one with cheap fabric and poor construction.

In your notebook or purse, keep a list for family members: their shoe, shirt, and clothing sizes, plus their favorite colors. Then when you run into a sale, you'll have the information at your fingertips.

	Shirts	Pants/Skirts	Dresses/Suits	Sweaters	Shoes
Husband					
Child					
Child					
Child					
Self					

Mother _____

Father _____

The same goes for furnishings in your house. If you're decorating or moving into a new house, keep a slip of paper or card in your purse that lists colors, measurements, and so on.

Life Expectancy of Appliances

gas range	13.5 years	washing machine	10.8 years
electric range	12.1 years	gas dryer	12.8 years
refrigerator	15.2 years	electric dryer	13.7 years
dishwasher	11.1 years		

A no-frost refrigerator will use more electricity than one that you must defrost from time to time. A side-by-side refrigerator will cost more to operate than one that has refrigerator on top, freezer on bottom (or vice versa). A freezer chest on the bottom and refrigerator on top makes the best use of energy-saving physics. (Hot air rises, so the colder unit on the bottom will work less to maintain its frigid temperatures.) A chest-type freezer is more efficient than an upright freezer. (And if you defrost it yourself, you'll save even more.) Small toaster-ovens are more efficient for a married couple or small family than the large oven used for cooking small quantities of food.

Be an informed consumer. Check your local library for the yearly consumer's buying guides. They list and compare similar products and tell you the good and bad features of each. Libraries usually carry monthly publications that keep consumers informed on money-saving products. Back issues can be checked out.

The government publishes free brochures on over two hundred consumer-related subjects. Write to Consumer's Information Catalog, Pueblo, Colorado, 81009. Ask for their free catalog, and then you can write for the pamphlets that interest you most. They include do-it-yourself and how-to projects from canning to weaving to building your own stone wall or fireplace.

Savings and Loans

In spite of the fact that inflation causes a $1.00 purchase today to require $1.50 in a few years to buy the same goods, having a savings plan can help. Take a look at the figures below. If you saved $10 a week in a 5½% savings account that compounds interest daily, you would have $535 at the end of the year. Think what you could do with that extra money. Pay for medical or dental bills? Refurbish or redecorate? Buy clothes?

	Weekly Savings		
Years	$10	$20	$30
1	$ 535	$1,070	$1,604
2	$1,100	$2,200	$3,299
3	$1,697	$3,393	$5,090

What does a loan really cost? First of all, if you were to go to a bank for a loan, you'd have to prove you have a regular income. The bank won't risk investing in you unless they know that they have some way of getting their money back in the event you default.

Suppose you were buying a car. With an average interest rate of 12% (most revolving charge accounts can go as high as 18%), here is an example of how much you'd pay in monthly costs as well as the total finance charge. In the chart following you'll see what it actually costs to borrow $1,000 for one year. Notice that if you choose to pay a smaller monthly payment over a longer period of time, your total finance charge mushrooms.

12% interest rate

Loan of $1,000	1 yr.	2 yrs.	3 yrs.	4 yrs.
Monthly Payment	$89	$ 47	$ 33	$ 26
Total Finance Charge	$66	$130	$196	$264

What about your charge accounts? How long have you been trying to pay them off? That $30 skirt you bought nine months ago—how much is it really costing you? At 18% per year interest, that $300 appliance will cost you an additional $54. Whenever possible, pay off your charge accounts before finance charges are applied. Your total debt from credit should not exceed one month's salary.

Record Keeping

Stationery or variety stores carry handy organizers that can be used to keep sales slips, warranties and pamphlets that come with appliances. Look for an organizer with individual compartments labeled "Small Appliances," "Large Appliances," "Home Furnishings," "Lawn Care Products," etc. Then when your picture tube goes out, you have a record of where it was purchased and how long the warranty is in effect. This is a much better system than tossing such information loose in a drawer. This information will come in handy should you need to report losses to insurance companies. You'll know exactly how much the item cost when it was new.

Keeping a box or file for insurance policies is essential. You should also record the policy number and your agent's phone number on the outside of the file. Better yet, record all that information on one sheet of paper so you have a quick reference for emergencies. Give your husband a copy to keep at work in case your original is lost. Other information to include on the sheet: account numbers for banks, insurance policy numbers, Social Security numbers, credit cards, driver's license numbers, car registration numbers.

Important Money Numbers

ACCOUNT NUMBERS

Your bank _____ Bank phone _____

Savings Account No. _____

Checking Account No. _____

Safe-Deposit Box No. _____

Life Insurance Policy name and no. _____

Agent _____ Agent's phone number _____

Auto Insurance Policy name and no. _____

Agent _____ Agent's phone number _____

Homeowners Policy name and no. _____

Agent _____ Agent's phone number _____

Medical Insurance name and no. _____

Phone _____

Your Social Security no. _____

Spouse's Social Security no. _____

Children's Social Security no. _____

_____

_____

CREDIT CARD NUMBERS

   (Name)   (Number)

_____ _____

_____ _____

_____ _____

_____ _____

MOTOR VEHICLE INFORMATION

Car License Plate no. _____ Registration no. _____

Car License Plate no. _____ Registration no. _____

Your Driver's License no. _____ Spouse's _____

  Always store your bills in the same place for easy access. Have a regular day each week (or month) designated as bill-paying day. Plan a special treat (coffee cake or your favorite dessert) to reward yourself when the job is finished.
  Here's an idea to help you categorize your bills when they come in. Make four divisions in a notebook that has pocket dividers. Label the pockets "first week," "second week," and so on. As soon as the mail comes, open each bill. When is it due? Have a calendar next to your organizer. If you file each bill under the week it's due, you won't have to physically handle that bill again until it's time to pay it. (You lose valuable time whenever you handle a bill or document more than once.) When payday comes, pull out the bills for that week and write checks for them. You'll never be caught off guard by an overdue bill.

FAMILY FINANCIAL CYCLE

*mild financial demands **moderate ***heavy

1. Early Marrieds (no children) * to **
2. Preschool Family ** to ***
3. Grade School * to **
4. High School ** to ***
5. College *** to ****!
6. Empty Nest *
7. Old Age and Retirement * to **

1. *Early Marrieds.* You're just starting out. If you both work, you won't notice the financial strain as much. Whenever possible, try to live on one person's salary and put the rest in savings. (You're getting ready to face the next phase which is heavier, and yet you may only have one salary to live on.) It is possible to avoid buying a washing machine at this stage, but as soon as you get a house or start having babies, then you really need one.

2. *Preschool Family.* Suddenly you feel as if you will never get ahead. Money goes out as fast as it comes in. Heavy credit buying is tempting and in some cases almost the only way to get through this period. The four or five years when the children are small seem to be the time families want to upgrade their decor of "early hodge-podge" and get something to last through the school years.

This is the time when you can't live without a washing machine and a dependable refrigerator. You may have moved out of an apartment into a house. Your heating bills go up. Heavy stress both emotionally and financially. But hang in there. Grade school is coming and you'll get a breather for a few years.

3. *Grade School.* The children's shoes and clothing seem to wear out before they outgrow them. By comparison, however, your clothing costs will be less than for preschool years. Your washing machine has paid for itself and

should last until the high school years. The furniture is still holding out and except for the usual childhood diseases, everyone's health will be generally good. Some families experience more medical bills for childhood injuries. Children may start sports or music instruction. By and large you find things going smoothly and may think the rest of life will be the same. You're in for a shock, however. This is the lull before the next financial storm.

4. *High School.* The furniture is probably on its last leg, literally. All the jumping and rough play has worn through upholstery and slipcovers. The damage to carpeting from pets and traffic has taken its toll. The washing machine is starting to huff and puff and so are you. You'd best make the changes now in light of future college expenses. If you buy secondhand appliances, you may be able to make it through the college years without having to worry about another major appliance purchase. If you can afford a really good machine now, it may last you through your empty nest and retirement years. The kids, especially boys, outgrow clothes so rapidly. Buy good clothes on sale at the end of one season and buy the sizes which they will grow into by the next year. The kids want to use the car, so up goes your gasoline and fuel costs, not to mention the insurance rates.

5. *College Years.* You are getting letters from college: "Mom and Dad, send money!" Mother may have decided to reenter the work force to keep the kids in school. The kids save their laundry to bring home with them on weekends. If you can just get through these years, there's a time awaiting you when the salary will allow for cash to travel, invest in retirement property, or spend on the first grandchild.

6. *Empty Nest.* The home once bustling with children is quiet. You may decide to go back to work to keep your mind busy now that mothering duties are in the background. Tired of the decor that once thrilled you as a young couple, you redecorate and invest in some really good pieces. The kids get your castoffs. You have more

time for leisure, entertainment, travel, sports, etc. You're making retirement plans and may have purchased some land. A few old appliances are breathing their last, a reminder that things can't go unchanged forever.

7. *Old Age and Retirement.* Happy day! You're enjoying grandchildren and trips to visit the kids. Moving from a large, paid-for home to a smaller living unit may be a consideration; however, you may hate to think about having to make mortgage payments again. (If interest rates are sky-high, you may be wise to stay put.) This is the time to make sure your nutritional and exercise requirements are being met. If you're not in good health, your income will be devoured by medical costs. (At this point you may be muttering to yourself, "If I'd known I was going to live *this* long, I'd have taken better care of myself!") Some retirees decide to return to the work force either to augment Social Security or to keep mind and body stimulated.

CHAPTER 10

Simple Home Repairs

CHALLENGING THE HEART

Woe is me! When you are caught in the jaws of misfortune . . . when everything turns sour . . . when what you wanted most slips from your grasp . . . that's when an otherwise smooth-running day turns lumpy. As Job said, "Man is born for trouble, as sparks fly upward" (5:7).

Consider one of the common tragedies of life: a broken tooth. You go to the dentist, and he discovers other dental problems while repairing your simple chipped tooth. Part of you groans, "Why did I even come here? I didn't want to hear about the other problems!" Take a car to the repairman and the same thing happens. On such days you can become overwhelmed at the misfortune that seems to lurk everywhere.

Let's take a new look at trouble. This may be the first time in your life that you learn to fix a leaky faucet, repair a broken plug, or discover that you can survive in the world without Dad, friend or husband to rescue you from calamity. (This is significant, since statistics show that more women are choosing to remain single longer. More women are heading the family unit as single parents. And finally, women need to know how to survive the experience of widowhood.)

How can trouble help you? Consider some of the following ways.

Trouble may be a way of guarding you from grave dangers further ahead. Health problems alert you to possible life-robbing threats later on. Taking care of yourself now may save your life later. Similarly, discovering a serious defect in your car before an accident occurs may save your life.

Trouble may be the means for causing you to reexamine your values and/or priorities. Suppose you are turned down for a hefty promotion. If you had received that promotion, would your moral values have been threatened or challenged seriously over a period of time? Would you have had to give up Sunday worship? Would you have had to sacrifice too much time away from loved ones? Would you have been asked to do something that could be classified as unethical? In hindsight, you may be thankful for the disappointment that caused you to rethink your values and dreams.

Trouble may show you how much you need others. Our society applauds the efforts of helping others, but inadequately prepares us to accept help from others. The truth is, we were not created to be totally self-sufficient. God built human need for others into the world system. So the next time your car stalls or gets a flat tire, just think: *someone out there has a gift for fixing those things.* You're allowing that person the opportunity to use his/her God-given gifts for your benefit. Your weakened state when trouble strikes is God's window of opportunity to show you that He can call others to meet your needs.

Trouble may be a means of rerouting you to a better circumstance. Trouble can be a "detour arrow" if you'll look for the signs. Think of the young girl who was disappointed in love. How she pleaded with God to make this young man notice her. A year later she wrote in her diary, "Night on night I prayed on end to win him for my dear. Thank heavens, God was occupied with something else that year!"

Trouble develops patience and builds faith. When you're flat on your back, the only way to look is UP! God can use your troubles to make an "appointment" with you.

Trouble builds compassion for others. Until you've had a problem, you have some difficulty developing genuine sympathy and empathy for others. For example, if you've experienced the loss of a loved one, then you have a special tenderness and sensitivity for others who are going through the experience. You've been there. You know. Then, when you put a consoling arm around your friend, the touch conveys more than words can say. "Blessed be the . . . God of all comfort; who comforts us in all our affliction so that we may be able to comfort those who are in any affliction" (2 Corinthians 1:3, 4).

Trouble teaches practical skills. Your mother gets sick. She can't care for you, so you learn to do your own laundry and fix some meals. Your basic survival skills develop when trouble strikes. What have you learned as a result of your troubles?

Prayer: Give me courage to face life's frustrations and tragedies, knowing that You can work through them to help me grow. Give me the self-confidence I need to learn new skills, and may I use them to help others as well as myself. Amen.

CHALLENGING THE HANDS

This chapter includes some helpful information on the use of basic tools needed for home repair jobs. Before you schedule your meeting, poll the group members for suggestions of the kinds of skills they would like to learn. Then search for one or more handypersons who can teach and demonstrate those techniques to your group. If possible, provide materials for practice in repairs with each person getting hands-on experience in at least two projects.

USING BASIC TOOLS

Hammer

A medium weight (12-13 ounces) claw hammer is good for general purposes.

- Hold a hammer near the end of the handle for more hitting power. To start a nail, hold it in place and tap it gently a few times until it is firmly set. Hit it straight in. (Fig. 1)

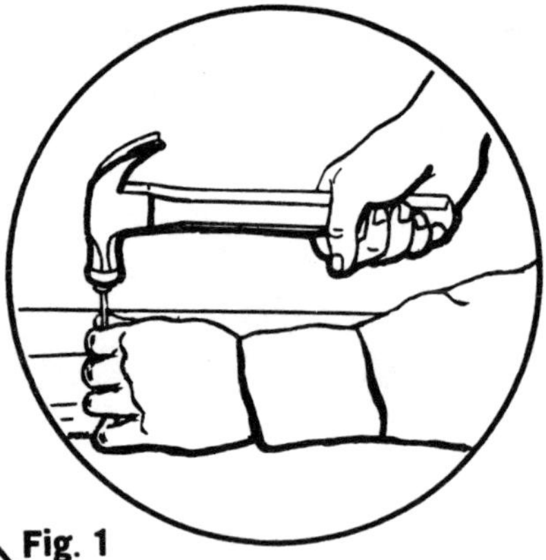

Fig. 1

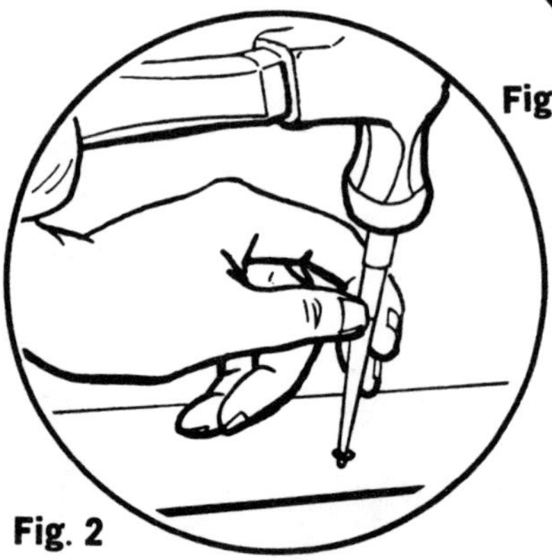

- To avoid hammer marks on the wood, use a nail set(Fig. 2) or another nail to drive a nail the last one-eighth inch into the wood.

Fig. 2

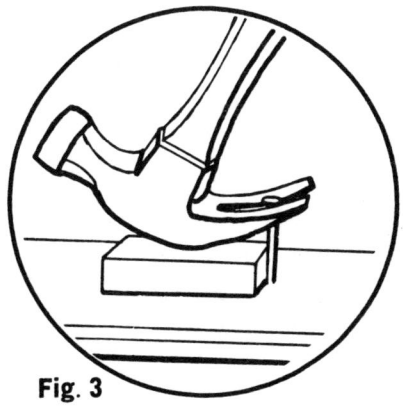

Fig. 3

- To remove a nail use claw end of hammer. Place a small block of wood under the head of the hammer to avoid marking the wood (Fig. 3).

Screwdriver

You need two types of screwdrivers for household repairs: **Straight blade** (Fig. 4), and **Phillips** (Fig. 5). Both come in various sizes. The blade of the screwdriver should fit the slot in the screw. (Fig. 6)

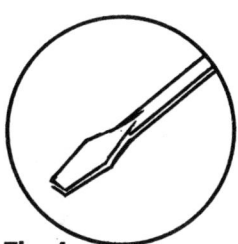

Fig. 4

Fig. 5

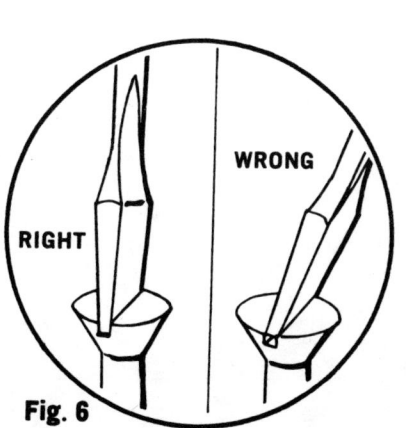

RIGHT   WRONG

Fig. 6

- When using the screwdriver, push against the head of the screw as you turn it. (Fig. 7)

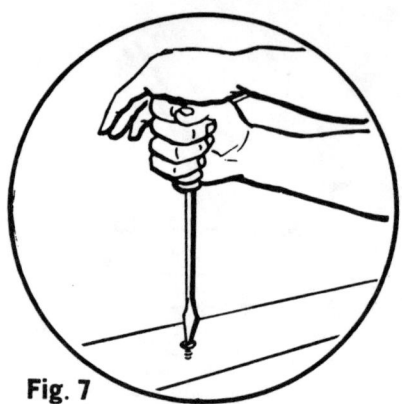

Fig. 7

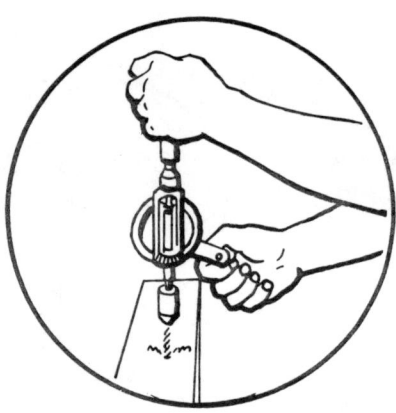

Fig. 8

- It's easier to put a screw into wood if you make a hole first with a nail or drill. (Fig. 8) Rub wax or soap on the screw threads to make it go in easier.

Pliers

A **slip joint pliers** can be used for many jobs around the house. (Fig. 9)

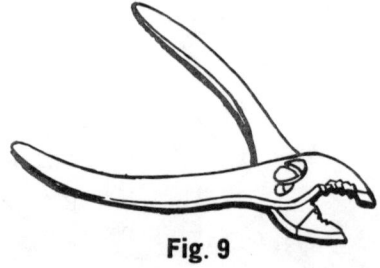

Fig. 9

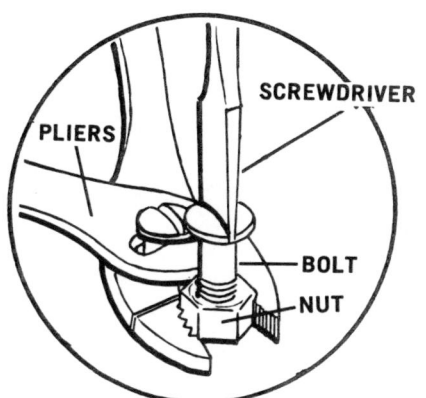

Fig. 10

- Use pliers to hold a nut while you turn a bolt with a screwdriver. (Fig. 10)

- Use it to remove nails or brads. Pull the nail out at the same angle it was driven in. Use small blocks under the pliers if you need leverage. (Fig. 11)

Fig. 11

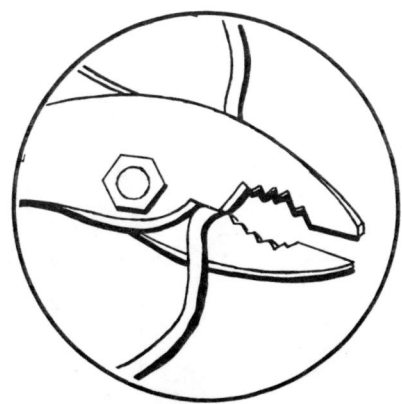

- Use it to bend or cut wire or to straighten a bent nail. (Fig. 12)

Fig. 12

- Use it to turn nuts. Wrap tape or cloth around the nut to avoid scratching it. (Fig. 13)

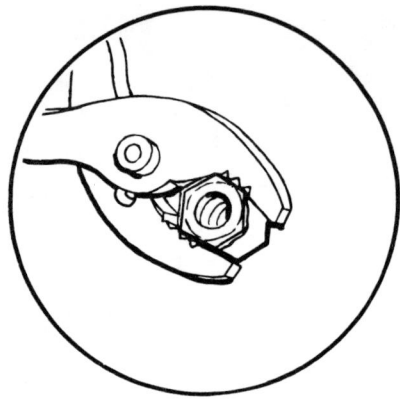

Fig. 13

An **adjustable wrench** (Fig. 14) is adjustable to fit different sizes of nuts.

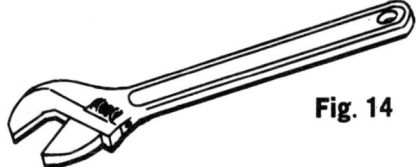

Fig. 14

- If a nut is hard to loosen, apply a few drops of penetrating oil or kerosene. (Fig. 15) Let it soak a couple of hours or overnight. If the wrench has a tendency to slip off, try turning it over.

Fig. 15

Handsaw

A handsaw (Fig. 16) with about 10 teeth to the inch is good for most household work. (Fig. 17)

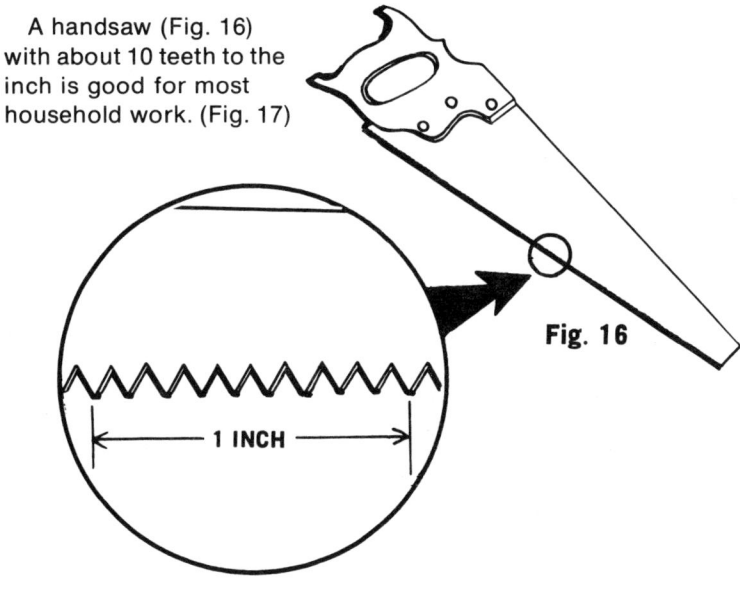

Fig. 16

Fig. 17

- Mark where you want to cut. Pull the saw back and forth several times to start a groove. Let the weight of the saw do the cutting at first. If you are sawing a board, it will be easier if you support it and hold it firmly near where you're cutting. (Fig. 18)

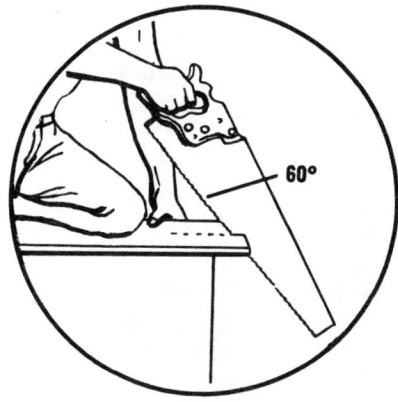

Fig. 18

CHAPTER 11

Caring for Silver, Linens and China

CHALLENGING THE HEART

" 'Let us rejoice and be glad and give the glory to Him, for the marriage of the Lamb has come and His bride has made herself ready.' And it was given to her to clothe herself in fine linen, bright and clean; for the fine linen is the righteous acts of the saints" (Revelation 19:7, 8).

Who doesn't love a wedding? A wedding is such a happy time of celebration and feasting. The Bible verses we just read speak of the Lord Jesus Christ as the "Lamb" who is awaiting His bride. Did you know that *you* are that bride? Specifically, the Bible says that the bride is to be the church, and the church is the believers.

Imagine, even if you never marry on earth, one day you will be a bride for Jesus! How exciting that day will be. What will it be like when the Bridegroom (Jesus) comes? We don't know all the details, but we do know that God's biggest concern for you and me is that He wants us to be ready.

The Bible verse speaks of the bride's linens as the symbol of righteousness and purity before God. How does a bride demonstrate righteousness? Picture a gracious bride-hostess who attends to her guests as she mingles during the reception. She receives honor and attention, of course, but her most important duty is to make all her guests feel welcome. She is serving others even though she is in a position to have others serve her.

Some of you remember when every young girl wanted a "hope chest" to fill in anticipation of her future marriage. She made and collected items for her trousseau: linens for table and bed, silver pieces, lace, towels, and possibly a few family heirlooms. Many girls made or decorated these items using handcraft or needlework skills. Eventually, the tradition of the hope chest faded and with it went many of the arts and handworks skills. Who knew how to add decorative lace trim to pillowcases? Who remembered how to quilt? Instead, girls waited until they became engaged and asked for Tupperware and permanent press! If someone gave them fine silver pieces or real linens, they had no idea how to care for such things. So the pieces were stored away to tarnish and attract moths.

There is a parable hidden here. Linens and silver need to be used, not hidden away. Silver takes on a luster and patina that is lovely—but only if it is used. Regular polishing keeps tarnish under control. It is the same in life. If you have a talent or gift or an ability to help others but you choose to store it on a forgotten shelf, your gift becomes rusty. The longer you refuse to use the gift, the harder it is to polish it when the occasion comes to bring it forth.

Recently, many people have shown a renewed interest in the beautiful and useful items our grandparents took for granted: antique furniture, utensils, handcrafts, needlework. They are collecting items from Grandma's attic, Grandpa's barn, garage sales, and auctions—instant heirlooms! There is once again a need to know how to care for and enjoy the long-lasting beauty of china, silver and linens.

Could you polish some silver, iron some linens, and surprise your family with a beautiful table setting this week? When they ask, "What's this for, is it somebody's birthday or something?" you can say, "No special occasion, except that you're all special!"

Prayer: Remind me, Lord, to keep my life shiny and bright and clean. Remind me to think about my spiritual gifts, my natural talents and my material possessions in unselfish ways. Help me to use my God-given abilities to make others happy. Prod me if I get careless about the things I possess so I'll be mindful of them. Amen.

CHALLENGING THE HANDS

Suggested Activities

1. Have a polishing bee! Look around the house for tarnished pieces of silver. Bring them to class and enjoy the friendly visiting that makes the minutes of polishing pass quickly. Choose at least one piece that is slightly tarnished and one that really needs work. At the end of the class, display your lustrous work on a dark tablecloth.

2. Have each member bring four small pieces of linen (napkins, table scarves, etc.). Have ready-mixed bowls of laundry starch: light, medium, heavy. Iron one piece with no starch. Then dip another in light starch, another in medium, and a final piece in heavy starch. Put in the dryer until damp dry, then iron. This will give the members hands-on experience in starching and ironing linens and allow them to compare the various degrees of starch for their own use.

3. Invite two or three women to set up sample tables using their linens, china, glassware and flatware. You might want to have one table for a breakfast setting, another for an informal lunch, another for a family dinner using everyday linens, another for a more formal setting.

4. Invite someone who knows how to make unusual designs with napkin folding to show you how it's done (holiday napkin folding, napkin folding for formal dinners, unusual shapes with napkins). Bring large dinner napkins—formal size works best. Make sure they are moderately to heavily starched.

CARING FOR SILVER

Why is silver so valuable?

Can you imagine using silver and gold to barter for food or safe passage out of a war-torn country? In hard economic times or in times of war, that's exactly what has happened. One always hopes that history will not repeat itself in our lifetime.

On the other hand, sometimes the economic climate of the world will cause the price of gold and silver to skyrocket, as it did in the early 1980's. With gold valued at over $500 an ounce, many people stood in line for hours for the chance to sell their jewelry and silverware. Others, fearing increased theft, hid their family pieces in some very unusual places. Imagine the horror of discovering that boxes of throwaways or donations to charity had held a favorite candelabra or cream and sugar set!

The price of a silver piece is determined by two things: the actual cost of the silver plus the value of the item it is used in. (In the case of antiques, the price may go very high.) If you were to sell a decorative piece to a silversmith, you might not get what it is "really worth" because he is interested only in the weight of the silver and its value.

Silver and gold have value no matter what country you live in. And if you can look beyond its use for investment, for entertainment, for industry or science, you will have to admit that silver is just beautiful. That, above all, is perhaps the best reason to admire and enjoy it.

What's the difference between sterling silver and silver plate?

Sterling is pure silver with the addition of a small quantity of copper or other metal to give it strength. For a piece to be stamped "sterling" or "925" it must have 925 parts of silver to no more than 25 parts of copper or other metal. In the United States these markings are engraved on sterling pieces. In Europe a series of three or four different marks are stamped to show the date, origin, etc.

Silver plate is not as expensive as sterling silver. Composed of layers of silver electrically deposited, some silver plate is triple or quadruple plated and may come with a lifetime guarantee. Should any of the layers wear thin, it is possible to have the piece replated.

It should be mentioned that if you want the look of silver and your budget is limited, silver plate will serve you just as well. If you own sterling, it can be appraised (valued) by a reputable jeweler and should be listed on your insurance policy.

Unless you have family pieces or heirlooms, starting a place setting of silver at today's prices will leave you in a state of shock. The family pieces that were very affordable for your grandmothers and great grandmothers, today might cost thousands of dollars.

Is there any way to find a "good buy" on silver? Keep your eyes sharpened for garage and yard sales. Silver plated pieces are regularly sold for much less than retail. Watch for jewelry store sales that occur periodically. You might pick up a piece for 30%-50% of its retail price.

Today's brides are not likely to receive "service for eight" or even service for two! Collecting serving pieces, napkin rings, and other small items might be more practical if you're just starting out.

What causes tarnish? How can I protect against it?

Sulphur compounds in the air and in certain foods (eggs especially) cause silver to tarnish or turn black. Tarnish happens naturally to pieces exposed to air. Fortunately, it can be corrected by polishing and cleaning.

Pitting, on the other hand, is caused by moisture and salt. If you live in a humid climate or near the ocean, pitting is a real danger. If you use silver pieces to hold nuts and hors d'oeuvres, the salts and acids will also result in pitting if you don't carefully wash and dry after use. Pitting affects silver plate as well as sterling, although it seems to occur more frequently in the plated pieces.

Whichever kind of silver you own, don't be guilty of neglect. Don't allow foods to dry on the surfaces of utensils.

Ideally, silver pieces do better if they are completely kept away from humidity. A hutch or other display case which allows you to view pieces through glass windows will help keep tarnish to a minimum.

Whatever you do, DON'T wrap silver in tight-fitting plastic film or newspapers! The plastic or ink may become imbedded in the silver. A heavy-gauge plastic bag with a zipper-lock feature will do fine for storage, and you can expel some of the air before you seal it.

In addition to jewelry stores, department stores and mail-order catalogs often carry the special bags and storage cases for your silver. Or you can buy the treated fabric called Pacific cloth. It has a tarnish-inhibiting ingredient. This material is sold by the bolt or by the yard in fabric stores or through mail-order catalogs. You can make simple bags custom-fit for your pieces. If you live in a high humidity area and plan to store your pieces for a long time, add the additional protection of a plastic bag over the fabric bags.

Keep in mind that nothing short of vacuum packing will ensure an absolutely perfect, tarnish-free environment. It is expected that you will have to invest some time and effort to keep silver lustrous and beautiful.

How should I clean and polish my silver?

It is not advisable to put silver in the dishwasher. Harsh cleaners and high heat can erode minute amounts of silver.

Immediately after using your silver, before food has a chance to dry on it, wash it or put it to soak in warm, sudsy water. Don't put too many pieces in the sink at once. Keep forks separate from knives and spoons so the tines won't scratch the other pieces. Wash each piece separately, gently; rinse in hot water. Let drain a few moments; then rub dry with a lint-free cloth to prevent water spotting. (Your cloth will be more absorbent if you launder it *without* using fabric softener.) Let it air dry a few more minutes; then put it away.

When polishing your silver avoid using "instant" dip-type cleaners that contain harsh chemicals. When you polish, you are actually removing a minute layer of silver along with the tarnish. The stronger or more abrasive the cleaner, the more silver you will rinse down the drain. A mild cream or paste polish, a soft cloth or sponge, and some old-fashioned elbow grease are the safest, surest tools for polishing silver.

Follow the directions on your cleaning product. Rub each piece in one direction only, just as you would polish wood furniture with the grain. Wash it in mild suds, rinse, and dry thoroughly with a lint-free cloth.

Work over a counter or table, cushioned with towels. If you drop that silver dish, vase, or candlestick, you will surely dent or scratch it. Silver is soft!

Treated polishing cloths work best for touch-ups on mildly tarnished pieces. Some jewelers recommend using a treated cloth once a week or so to keep pieces tarnish free.

Silver is meant to be enjoyed! Plan to use your good things at least three or four times a year. If you have trouble with occasional fingerprints appearing as tarnish marks, you'll know you are not using your silver often enough.

CARING FOR LINENS

What is a "true" linen?

True linens are made from flax. The quality of the flax and the processing determines the softness of the resulting fabric. A high-quality linen is expensive. In fact, the high cost of linens has caused many consumers to reach for the lower priced synthetics and blends. By blending flax with cotton, rayon, or polyester, some of the best features of each allow for greater choices in performance.

What are the differences between true linen and a synthetic or blend?

True linens are far more durable, sometimes lasting through two and three generations depending on frequency of use and care. True linens have a rich, luxurious feel. True linens release stains easier than modern blends.

However, the cost of linens is very high for most budgets. Considerable time is needed to properly care for true linen.

On the other hand, modern permanent-press linens are affordable for most budgets. At the price, you can afford to have more than one nice item. They require little or no ironing.

However, they stain easily. The stains are frequently stubborn and do not readily come out. The life expectancy of permanent press is much shorter than linens. If you use your synthetic linens frequently, you may find the cost of replacements will end up higher than if you had invested in a good linen at the start.

How should I clean and care for my linens?

Immediately after use, check your tablecloths, napkins, towels, etc. for soil and stains. They must be pretreated *before* laundering. Refer to an up-to-date stain removal guide for proper treatment of lipstick, food, beverage and other stains. Methods will vary according to the type of stain and the fabric.

Once spots have been treated or removed, you're ready to launder. Use hot water for white, warm water for colored if you are laundering true linens. With permanent press, usually a warm-water wash with cool rinse is recommended. For true linens and most permanent press (whites and light colored) you may use a chlorine bleach. Always dilute the bleach before adding to wash water. Then add the linens.

The most common cause of yellowing or graying of fabric is improper laundering (not enough detergent) and/or water that isn't hot enough. Also be sure all detergent is thoroughly rinsed out.

There's nothing more luxurious than the feel of crisply starched tablecloths and dinner napkins. Even permanent-press articles benefit by light starching and a touch-up with the iron. Use concentrated liquid or powdered starch and dilute according to directions. Use a medium mixture first if you're experimenting. (Spray starch is convenient, but expensive, and it doesn't give the same "professional" results. If you have just a few small items, buy and mix regular concentrated starch and pour it into a clean trigger-spray bottle.) Small items can be hand dipped and wrung or put back to spin dry. Large items can be starched right in the machine using the final rinse cycle. Check your machine instruction book.

Put linens in the dryer on warm or permanent-press setting. *Check them frequently and remove from dryer while still damp.* If you don't have time to iron them right away, roll them up in a plastic bag and put them in the freezer until you're ready to iron.

Set the iron carefully on "cotton," "linen" or the proper synthetic setting. It shouldn't be necessary to use steam. Iron on the wrong side, especially with damask. Modern, lightweight irons do not retain high temperatures well, and you must press with a heavy hand, which can be very tiring. If possible, borrow Grandma's old, heavy dry iron. It retains heat well, and the weight of the iron does the hard work for you.

If you use too much starch or your iron is too hot, scorching will result. If it does, treat it by soaking in bleach and laundering again.

Why does my linen have so many wrinkles?

First, you may have put your tablecloths away while they were slightly damp. Use a dry setting on your iron to remove the last traces of dampness. After ironing a section, wait a few seconds and feel with the back of the hand. Is it still damp to the touch after the heat has left the fabric? If so, iron some more.

The second cause of wrinkles is improper storage. Unless you roll your cloths around a cardboard tube, you'll have fold and crease lines when you remove your linens from the drawer or shelf.

Better yet, invest in an inexpensive dowel rod (available at craft shops or hardware stores) that can be suspended in a closet. Or drape your large tablecloths over a strong, padded hanger.

CARING FOR CHINA

What kind should I buy?

"China" is used loosely to describe many different kinds of dishes. "Real" china is considered to be very expensive and fragile compared to pottery, stoneware, and everyday, durable tableware.

Most people choose one set of dishes (settings for four to eight) from less expensive ceramic, pottery, or earthenware in addition to collecting settings of fine china. The most practical advice for anyone selecting everyday china is: choose from "open stock." This means, if any of your pieces break or chip, they can be replaced a piece at a time, and open stock pieces will usually be available for several years.

If you cannot afford to have a second set of china for company or special occasions, consider a plain white for everyday. It can be dressed up and accessorized with lovely table linens to look extra special. You could pick up small plates (salad or dessert size) in florals or designs to rest on top of your white dinner plate, to change the mood for the occasion. This eliminates the need to have a complete set of special-occasion china, and you can find sellout or discontinued items to use as these accent pieces.

Earthenware: Pottery and ceramic ware that is heavier than porcelain or bone china. Durable, less resistant to breakage than fine china, it is a good choice for everyday use. (Some pieces are ovenproof, which means they won't crack when exposed to high oven temperatures.)

Porcelain: White, hard, translucent ceramic ware, usually glazed. It is made from pure clay to which a little of the more fusable feldspar is added. Cost varies depending on the composition and method of manufacturing.

Bone China: By the addition of bone ash to porcelain, this china is equally beautiful and more resistant to breakage. Bone china is considered a permanent, lifelong possession. Famous names in bone china are: Spode, Wedgwood, Royal Doulton and Minton. All are produced in England. America also boasts some equally fine bone china: Haviland, Castleton, Lenox.

Here is a guide to the basic items necessary for two people. Eventually you will probably acquire service for four, six, or eight.

- 6 soup/cereal bowls
- 4 dinner plates
- 4 salad plates
- 8 cups and saucers
- 1 salt and pepper set
- cream pitcher and sugar bowl
- 1 casserole dish
- 1 serving platter
- 1 serving bowl

What is the difference between cut glass and crystal?

Cut glass is generally a more informal glass, although some lovely pieces are now made in less expensive glassware. Ornate designs or simple marks may be "cut" with a special wheel to produce the distinctive cut glass appearance.

Crystal contains lead and is therefore heavier than glass. The lead produces a clarity and sparkle. The thinner the glass, usually the more expensive it is. A characteristic "singing" can be heard if a wet finger quickly traces the rim of the goblet or glass.

How should I care for my fine china and crystal?

If you have a dishwasher and your pieces are labeled "dishwasher safe," use the china and crystal setting. If your machine does not have such a setting, don't risk using the dishwasher.

If you wash by hand, wash each piece separately. Don't put many pieces in the same water together; they bump and chip too easily. Lay an absorbent towel on the work surface and allow the pieces to drip dry for a minute. Then remove the remaining moisture using a soft, lint-free cloth. The less handling the better. Diapers make fantastic wiping cloths!

If your china or glassware has gold around the rims, wash it first. *Never wash it in the same water in which you have just washed silver.* A chemical reaction can take place that will remove some of the gold.

The best way to store china and crystal is in a china cabinet made especially for that purpose. If you must keep your china in a cupboard or closet, save the original packing boxes to store them in. Nest the cups in individual sections provided (never stack them!). Don't stack plates or bowls without placing sheet foam or other cushioning material between each one. Storage units made from quilted fabric can be purchased at department stores and through catalogs. They will protect your fine china and crystal and keep it clean.

CHAPTER 12

Entertaining at Home

CHALLENGING THE HEART

A missionary in Africa tells the story of a pride of lions and its aging king. When an old lion can no longer keep up with the hunt or fight to keep his position in the pride, the lions do not abandon him. Instead, they give him a new job.

The old king is positioned on one side of the hunting area. The young lions hide in the bushes and thickets on the other side. When an antelope appears, the old king's job is to roar loudly. The roar scares the antelope so much that the poor creature runs in the opposite direction. You guessed it! He runs right into the clutches of the young hunter lions.

When we run away from something that frightens us, we often run into deeper trouble. If we run long enough and hard enough, we can become ill or develop crippling phobias.

Suppose you were afraid of water. If you gave in to that fear instead of overcoming it by learning to swim, you might drown someday.

Many people have fear of being rejected or unpopular. Some take their fear a step farther by building invisible "fences" around themselves for protection. Some might become "stay-at-homes." Some might become antisocial or develop irritating habits that ensure their solitude.

What kinds of activities or situations do you fear? Make a list. Do any of these fears cause others to avoid you? Find a trusted friend or counselor to help you map out a plan of attack to overcome your particular fear. Remember that "God has not given us a spirit of timidity, but of power and love and discipline" (2 Timothy 1:7).

Prayer: Father, I need help in overcoming my fears. I can't do it alone. Show me other people in my life who can help me. Lead me to recognize that You have placed them in my life for that purpose. I know that I cannot develop courage by avoiding fearful situations. So help me to face them, secure in Your love. Amen.

CHALLENGING THE HANDS

Suggested Activities

An ideal way to end this series of programs on homemaking skills is to plan a party that involves many of the things you've learned.

Use some of your time this last session to organize your party. You may want to have it just for members, or if you're ambitious, invite spouses or friends. If you plan to repeat this series for another group of women, inviting them as your guests would be a great way to advertise the program and show them many of the things they will be learning.

Using your budgeting and meal planning skills, organize a potluck supper or luncheon that includes money saving main-dish recipes, homebaked bread, delicious homemade pies and beautifully decorated cakes!

Plan to bring samples of some of the things you've made as decorations or for display. For example, bring candles for the table, embroidered linens, flower arrangements, your good china, silver and crystal.

Of course, you will want to dress appropriately for the occasion and time of day and look your well-groomed best!

TIPS FOR INEXPERIENCED HOSTESSES

How do you feel about entertaining? Does it give you butterflies of excitement or dread? The more you entertain, the easier it becomes. And, of course, the parties that run the smoothest are those that are planned ahead. No, you don't have to have every second planned. Leave room for spontaneous interaction among your guests. But have a few things in mind to keep the party moving and avoid awkward moments.

For instance, try leaving "conversation starters" lying around to use if the conversation slumps: an unusual object on the coffee table, a scrapbook, a photo album, etc.

Do you have food placed in only one location? Instead,

have snacks available in a couple of rooms so you and your guests can move around. If you're serving a new food, have you tried the recipe on your family first? Then you'll know for sure whether that recipe for peanut butter parfait with chocolate sauce will be a hit or a bomb, and you'll save yourself from embarrassment.

New brides or birdes-to-be often make the mistake of thinking that the first homecooked meal must include all the family's favorites: like Aunt Bessie's famous steamed plum pudding, Grandma's scalloped potatoes, Mother's special wild rice stuffed capons. First thing you know, it's like having to orchestrate a Thanksgiving dinner—and you, just a rookie in the kitchen!

If you're a beginner, plan to serve just dessert or hors d'oeuvres. Save the family dinner until you feel comfortable with entertaining. If you must have a large group over, forget about the sit-down dinner. Serve buffet style. It's much easier, and your head will be less cluttered.

Do you know one of the biggest excuses for not entertaining? A well-meaning, would-be hostess says, "I'm dying to have you over, but I want to wait until I get some new china." Another favorite is, "I'm having the dining room redecorated, and I don't want to have anyone over until it's finished." (Usually the dining room is still "going to be decorated" two years later. She just never gets around to getting it started!)

Are you self-conscious about your small apartment or home? Do you worry that you don't have enough furniture to serve and seat everyone? Your guests are not coming to criticize your early hodgepodge decor. They're coming to spend time with you!

Here are some tips on entertaining when the surroundings are Spartan.

1. Make use of every room. If you had to, you could turn a bedroom into a fantasy out of an Arabian nights story. Suspend sheets from the ceiling, bring in the candlelight, turn on some soft music. It may sound a bit strange, but perhaps your imagination needs stretching! Some people

turn Ping-Pong tables into banquet tables. What could you use in new and different ways?

2. What about a picnic on the living room floor? Stretch out a checkered cloth, pack a picnic hamper, or, if you have a fireplace, roast hot dogs, pop corn, toast marshmallows over the flames. Serve mugs of hot chocolate.

3. Serve a Japanese or Chinese meal. Use the coffee table (or a large piece of plywood propped on cinder blocks) to serve the food. Sit on fluffy pillows on the floor. If necessary, buy the entree from a takeout restaurant. You add the rice, tea, and salad.

You needn't be a gourmet cook to entertain successfully. Even if you work outside the home and have little time to prepare foods from scratch, you can have informal or spur-of-the-moment gatherings.

Buy a nice ready-made coffee cake at the bakery or in the frozen foods section of your grocery store. Some are so exotic and rich, your guests will never notice the difference. And even if they do, tell them, "Having you here and enjoying your company is the most important thing to me."

Invite friends for a neighborhood potluck. You agree to supply the house, utensils, meat and beverages, while they bring the rest of the meal. In a day when food costs are skyrocketing, few will expect the red carpet treatment with filet mignons at your expense. So don't be too proud to accept an occasional donation to the meal from guests.

The important thing is not how long you labor over a hot stove, or how much money you spend, but rather, how much warmth and love you convey to your family and friends.

Do you feel unorganized? Do you entertain with good intentions, only to end up spending all your time in the kitchen away from your guests? You need a schedule!

Many cookbooks offer complete meals and cooking schedules to help you keep your preparations orderly and on time. Some women's magazines offer special features for the cook with little time. Most of those meals can be put together in less than an hour.

Plan to have at least two items on your menu as make-ahead or freeze-ahead foods. For example, assemble lasagna ahead and place it in the refrigerator. Assemble the salad (without the dressing) and store it in a plastic bag in the refrigerator until mealtime. Use store-bought rolls or heat-and-serve breads. Serve make-it-yourself ice cream sundaes for dessert. The flavor of many main dishes is improved when they are baked ahead and reheated. Do as much ahead as possible. Set your table the night before.

Do you get very nervous about entertaining? Consider sharing the hostess role with a friend. Two heads are better than one, and you can share the planning, execution, and the worry as well. Perhaps you would do better to have "spur-of-the-moment" entertaining. Some people discover that with less time to prepare, they entertain more casually and therefore can be more relaxed.

UNUSUAL ENTERTAINING

1. Have a mulligan stew party. Everyone brings something for the pot. Ask some to bring vegetables, some to bring extra cans of bouillon or soup stock. Play games while the kettle boils. Provide crackers and assorted breads.

2. A variation on the mulligan stew party is the miracle soup party. Everyone brings one can of soup. Do not bring any lobster or fishy soups! Miraculously, the flavors blend to produce a tasty soup. Vegetable soups and creamy soups do very well together. Ask each person to bring a favorite soup bowl or mug.

3. Gourmet popcorn feast. Pop corn at the party or ask guests to bring some ready-made. Using Larry Kusche's "Popcorn Cookery" (paperback cookbook), explore the hundreds of ideas for popcorn balls, appetizers, salads, desserts, sculptures, and unusual toppings. (Published by H. P. Books, P.O. Box 5367, Tucson, Arizona 85703)

MAKE A MENU-GUEST CARD FILE

On each card you include a list of menu items as well as the guests and the date you served the meal. This system will save you the embarrassment of serving the same meal to the same guests at a later date.

Develop at least two favorite "company" meals. Think of those food combinations that offer contrasts in taste, texture, and color. Try to concentrate on meals that run smoothly from the preparation point to the serving point. Write these menu plans on your cards. Instead of having to tax your recall every time a dinner needs to be planned, you can refer to your cards. No need to scratch your head and mumble, "What shall I fix?" It's right there on the card.

You will find that using the same two or three menus will get you through a year or two of entertaining. Each time you prepare the familiar recipes, your self-confidence will rise. You'll also notice that your shopping and food preparation time will become streamlined as repetition speeds you on your way.

front side

MENU

Swedish meatballs

hot rice

baby peas in butter sauce

cold marinated carrot salad

lemon bread

vanilla sundaes

chocolate-mint sauce

Guests	Date
Husband's boss	Aug. 1982
John and Martha	Dec. 1982

reverse side

Shopping List* (serves 4-6)

4 lbs. ground beef
1 box converted rice
frozen peas (2 pkgs.)
3 pkgs. carrots
1 bottle "catalina" dressing
onions
1 lb. butter
3 pkgs. yeast
white flour
mace
½ gallon vanilla ice cream
prepared chocolate sauce
bread crumbs

*check cupboards first for supplies on hand

**Inspirational Reading for Women
from Standard Publishing**

Frankly Feminine/God's Idea of Womanhood
by Gloria Hope Hawley

In spite of the claims of extremists on both sides of the womanhood issue, God's intentions for women are quite clear. You will appreciate Mrs. Hawley's intelligent and Scripturally-based approach to womanhood. **2969**

36 Devotionals for Women's Groups
by Idalee Vonk

"A Little Bending, a Little Stretching," "Making Decisions," "Mountains Out of Molehills," and "Here Lies a Christian" are among the titles of these 36 intriguing and stimulating devotionals. **3216**

Things Happen When Women Care
by Marie Frost

How one clever and resourceful woman used varied experiences and everyday circumstances to witness for her faith and bring others to Christ. **3217**

Available at your Christian bookstore or